INDIGENOUS COMICS AND GRAPHIC NOVELS

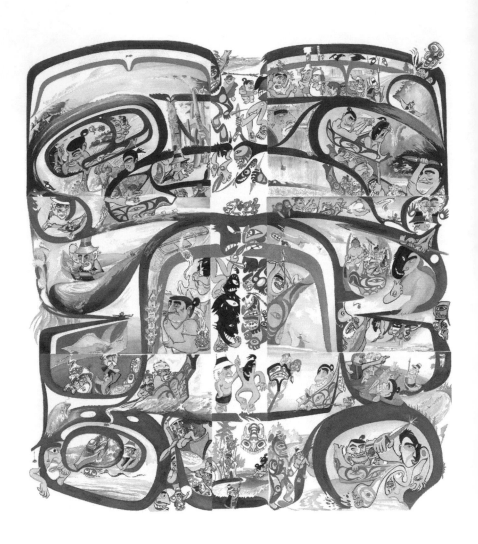

INDIGENOUS COMICS

AND GRAPHIC NOVELS

STUDIES IN GENRE

JAMES J. DONAHUE

UNIVERSITY PRESS OF MISSISSIPPI / JACKSON

The University Press of Mississippi is the scholarly publishing agency of the Mississippi Institutions of Higher Learning: Alcorn State University, Delta State University, Jackson State University, Mississippi State University, Mississippi University for Women, Mississippi Valley State University, University of Mississippi, and University of Southern Mississippi.

www.upress.state.ms.us

frontis image: *War of the Blink* by Michael Nicoll Yahgulanaas.

The University Press of Mississippi is a member of the Association of University Presses.

An earlier version of chapter 1 appeared as "Super Indians & the Indigenous Comics Renaissance," in *Graphic Indigeneity: Comics in The Americas and Australasia*, ed. Frederick Luis Aldama (Jackson: University Press of Mississippi, 2020), 254–72.

Library of Congress Cataloging-in-Publication Data

Names: Donahue, James J., 1974– author.
Title: Indigenous comics and graphic novels : studies in genre / James J. Donahue.
Description: Jackson : University Press of Mississippi, 2024. | Includes bibliographical references and index.
Identifiers: LCCN 2023043120 (print) | LCCN 2023043121 (ebook) | ISBN 9781496850492 (hardback) | ISBN 9781496850508 (trade paperback) | ISBN 9781496850515 (epub) | ISBN 9781496850522 (epub) | ISBN 9781496850539 (pdf) | ISBN 9781496850546 (pdf)
Subjects: LCSH: Comic books, strips, etc.—History and criticism. | Graphic novels—History and criticism. | Indigenous peoples in literature.
Classification: LCC PN6714 .D65 2024 (print) | LCC PN6714 (ebook) | DDC 791.5/352997—dc23/eng/20231206
LC record available at https://lccn.loc.gov/2023043120
LC ebook record available at https://lccn.loc.gov/2023043121

British Library Cataloging-in-Publication Data available

CONTENTS

INTRODUCTION

Why Indigenous Comics? Why Now?

3

CHAPTER 1

Super Problems Require Super Heroes:
Indigenous Superheroes and Their Communities

21

CHAPTER 2

Indigenous Travels in Space, Time, and Technology

53

CHAPTER 3

The Past Is Part of the Present:
Indigenous Historical Graphic Narratives

80

CHAPTER 4

Pushing the Boundaries of Representation:
Indigenous Experimental Graphic Narrative

111

CODA

But Wait, Isn't There More?

144

ACKNOWLEDGMENTS

149

CONTENTS

NOTES

151

REFERENCES

174

INDEX

185

INDIGENOUS COMICS AND GRAPHIC NOVELS

WHY INDIGENOUS COMICS?
WHY NOW?

Writing about the problems inherent in reading and analyzing Native American[1] literatures in his study *Red on Red: Native American Literary Separatism*, Craig Womack (1999; Creek/Cherokee) famously notes that Native American fiction is "vastly understudied" (81). In a similar vein, Hillary Chute (2017) opens her study *Why Comics? From Underground to Everywhere* by noting that, far too often, "the whole comics medium still often gets mistaken for its most popular genre: superheroes" (1). In different ways—and for different reasons—both scholars voice a very common complaint about both literary traditions: that they simply are not given the serious scholarly attention they deserve.[2] If we accept both positions—and I argue that we should—then Indigenous comics may occupy one of the most glaring lacunae in both popular reading and literary studies today. There are a number of reasons for this, which I will briefly discuss below. But more importantly, there are a growing number of outlets and scholars who are producing, marketing, promoting, teaching, and publishing scholarship on this fascinating and rapidly growing body of work.

When I began telling people about the research that eventually became this book, I was generally met with two types of responses. The first response was a mix of shock and wonder, with people expressing surprise that there are enough Indigenous comics and graphic novels to devote an entire book to (as opposed to a chapter in a book about Indigenous literatures[3]); I was commonly asked a version of the question, "Well, just how many Native comics artists can there be?" The second response was some version of "that's really cool" and either an offer of support from like-minded scholars or a reading list of best places to start. And I appreciated both responses, albeit for different reasons. All scholars love the second response; we all enjoy knowing that there will be an audience for our work (and, by extension, a growing audience for the authors that we are studying). However, the first response was just as encouraging because it demonstrated to me the necessity of the work, especially given that many of the people who responded that way were themselves scholars or students. And in this regard, I see this book as a means of support for the many Indigenous artists producing such amazing work: through my publishing, my teaching, and my networking in the field, I hope to continue to draw attention to these artists and their work. And just as importantly, I hope to use my continued work to demonstrate *why* this area of study is so important. And as will be made clear throughout this book, there is more to the study of Indigenous comics than mere representation. While representation is itself important, it is but the first step in a much longer process of understanding. I thus use this book to join the growing number of scholars who wish to make Indigenous artists more important in comics studies as well as those who wish to make comics more important in Indigenous studies.

However, if I'm being honest, I have to admit that, while certainly important, scholarly attention isn't the primary goal of Indigenous comics artists. Indigenous creators want the same thing all creators do: an audience. To reach that audience, Indigenous creators need distributors. And while some creators handle much of that work on their own, there are a few publishers and booksellers who are actively promoting the work of Indigenous comics creators and with great success.

• • •

The comics industry is massive and seemingly only getting larger. Given the unprecedented success of the Marvel Cinematic Universe (MCU) as well as the growing number of DC movies and TV series, popular interest in superhero stories drawn from comics seems insatiable. And while recognizing this fact may appear to fall into the trap that Chute complains about in *Why Comics?*, it certainly serves to highlight a level of popular interest that suggests comics—and those interested in them—are no longer on the fringes of popular culture. This interest is also evident in the increasing amount of shelf space that popular brick-and-mortar chain bookstores—such as Barnes & Noble in the United States and Indigo in Canada—now devote to graphic novels (which often now includes large sections devoted to manga as well). And while there are plenty of superhero titles on those shelves, a quick scan of the offerings reveals a wide variety of narratives for diverse audiences, produced by many of the large comics publishers, such as Image, Vertigo, and Dark Horse Books, in addition to the ever-popular Marvel and DC.

In short, comics have become far more popular over the past several years, and that popularity shows no signs of waning. However, that quick scan of bookstore shelves noted above will also undoubtedly give you a false impression of the diversity of titles being produced and of the diversity of creators producing such work. With very few exceptions,[4] Indigenous comics creators will not be found in those bookstores in part because most Indigenous authors are not being published by imprints with national distributions. However, some of these titles will be found in smaller, independent bookstores, which often specialize in carrying titles and lists from small presses and boutique publishers whose works are often not carried by large chain stores. One such example, located in Montréal, is the Librarie Drawn & Quarterly and their extension store La Petite Librarie Drawn & Quarterly, both of which carry a variety of graphic novels—in French as well as English—for readers of all ages. In addition to carrying many small press offerings—including but not limited to First Nations, Métis, and Inuit authors of fiction, poetry, and nonfiction as well as comics—these bookstores are also the storefront operation of *Drawn & Quarterly*, which describes itself as having "grown from a single-issue magazine to an internationally renowned publisher of the world's best cartoonists" (Drawn & Quarterly, n.d.), a publishing outlet for many emerging writers as well as such influential and popular comics authors as Lynda Barry, Daniel Clowes, and Chris Ware. Although not devoted exclusively to Indigenous writing, the Drawn & Quarterly stores and publishing house are committed to distributing the work of authors often not found in the chain bookstores noted above.

In a similar vein, Portage & Main Press—especially their imprint Highwater Press—are committed to producing titles by Indigenous authors in myriad genres, including comics and graphic novels.[5] Among its many titles and series produced by First Nations, Métis, and Inuit writers are the *7 Generations* series (which have been collected in a single volume) and the Tales from Big Spirit series, both of which were written by David Alexander Robertson (Swampy Cree), which I will discuss in more detail in chapter 3. Both of these series are explicitly advertised for use in the classroom, and a teacher's guide is available for both series. Additionally, one of the most recent titles I mention in the coda, Richard Van Camp's (Dogrib Tł̨chǫ) *Three Feathers*, is available in bilingual editions with English paired with Chipewyan, Cree, or Slavey. More than just a publishing house, Portage & Main is committed to promoting inclusivity in education. In addition to the teacher's guides available for many of their publications—which, I should note, are well worth popular consumption as well as educational use—the press offers a variety of lesson plans for over a dozen subject areas and grade levels, as well as books focused on inclusive educational practices, including Chelsea Vowel's (Métis) *Indigenous Writes: A Guide to First Nations, Métis & Inuit Issues in Canada*. This is one of the many titles in the Debwe Series, a series devoted to Indigenous writings in nonfiction and fiction as well as graphic novels.

Similarly, in the United States, Native Realities is devoted to publishing Native American authors, primarily but not exclusively those producing comics and graphic novels. Founded by Dr. Lee Francis IV (Laguna Pueblo), Native Realities is the corporation behind the Indigenous Comic Con, which debuted in Albuquerque, New Mexico, in 2016,[6] as well as Red Planet Books & Comics (now ATCG), which was the only brick-and-mortar store in the United States devoted to the sale of books, comics, and pop art from Indigenous creators. Dr. Francis has been tireless in his efforts (as noted on the now-defunct webpage) "to highlight the amazing work that Native and Indigenous folks are doing in and around pop culture and get folks excited to come visit our shop" (Red Planet Books & Comics, n.d.). Similarly, his popular moniker, "the Stan Lee of Native American comics," is more than just an honorific; Dr. Francis is also the writer behind *Sixkiller*, a new comic-book series, and *Ghost River: The Fall and Rise of the Conestoga*, both illustrated by Weshoyot Alvitre (Tongva). And like the late Stan Lee, Dr. Francis has helped shepherd, publish, and distribute a variety of comics titles, in print and e-book[7] formats, including various comics series, graphic novels, and anthologies. Series like *Hero Twins* by Dale Deforest (Navajo), as well as anthologies such as *Deer Woman* and the much-anticipated *Ghost River*,[8] reflect the variety of kinds of stories Dr. Francis has worked to create and promote, stories addressing Indigenous histories and futures, adaptations of traditional stories from diverse Indigenous nations, and works that reflect a variety of visual aesthetic styles.

Unfortunately, for all the great work Dr. Francis does to promote Indigenous comics artists, many working artists are still creating, publishing, and promoting their work largely by themselves. One such artist—whose work I will discuss in detail in chapter 1—is Theo Tso (Las Vegas Paiute), creator of the series *Captain Paiute: Indigenous Defender of the Southwest*, which he writes, illustrates, and distributes from his War Paint Studios (War Paint Studios, n.d.). In addition to selling his work online, he has also posted publicly to Facebook about personally bringing copies of his work to local bookstores for sale. And while there is a long history of do-it-yourself work in comics publishing—especially in the underground comics community—the multimillion-dollar comics industry could certainly do a much better job about diversifying the series and titles they offer and offering their support to up-and-coming artists. This is especially the case when it comes to series like *Captain Paiute*, a superhero story that (as I will discuss in chapter 1), would fit right alongside some of the most popular superhero series currently being produced by Marvel and DC. (And without question, the MCU would absolutely benefit from the inclusion of an Indigenous superhero, who would bring a new perspective to the largely white cast and appeal to an even wider audience.)

• • •

Just as Indigenous literatures are increasingly appealing to—and finding—popular audiences (online as well as in print), Indigenous authors are increasingly finding their way into literature curricula and syllabi across North America. As I have written elsewhere (Donahue, 2020b), I earned degrees in English from three different universities, and the first time I ever saw a work by an Indigenous author on a syllabus was during my PhD coursework: James Welch's *Fools Crow* in a PhD seminar on the American Historical Romance. Native American literature courses were few and far between in many English departments, and Indigenous writers rarely seemed to make an appearance on college syllabi in American literature survey courses. And while many anthologies—such as the ever-popular *Norton Anthology of American Literature*—include an increasing number of Native American authors in their tables of contents, many current syllabi for survey courses continue to ignore the work of Indigenous authors. It is obviously impossible to conduct a comprehensive study of all such courses that are currently being taught. And rather than hunt down specific examples that serve as a foil, I will note here that I searched the internet for representative syllabi while writing this introduction. I found several syllabi from various universities posted online. The very first that came up in my search—for a survey course run at a mid-sized state university in a large state—included fifty-eight authors, only one of whom was Native American. (Further, she was one of the few authors to be covered either in one day or for which only one short work was to be read.) Another syllabus—for a survey course at a small, liberal arts college—included twenty-eight authors, none of whom were Native American. A third—for a course at a large community college—included three Native American authors out of thirty-three; all three were covered in one week (out of sixteen). These syllabi were all for courses that ran in 2017 and were three of the top four hits in my search. (The fourth was for a syllabus that did not include a reading list.) While I have no doubt that exceptions exist, it seems fairly common for such survey courses to minimize the importance of literature produced by Indigenous authors.

Internet searches for courses in "Native American literature and the graphic novel" similarly demonstrated that Indigenous comics artists are rarely included on such college syllabi. While courses in Native American and First Nations literatures have now become standard at many universities throughout the United States and Canada, those courses rarely include works by graphic novelists, including those whose works (as we saw above) are clearly aimed at and produced for classroom usage. (Only one of the top ten syllabi included in my internet search included the work of a comics author: *Red: A Haida Manga* by Michael Nicoll Yahgulanaas [Haida]. Interestingly, of the top ten results for my internet search for courses on the graphic novel, Yahgulanaas was the only Indigenous author included on one of the syllabi. And for good reason; as we will see in chapter 4, Yahgulanaas's work is an aesthetic, political, and cross-cultural tour de force.) Similarly, academic studies in both fields largely ignore the work of Indigenous comics artists. Most academic studies in comics and graphic novels—even if they include chapters on the works of other nonwhite creators—do not discuss the rapidly growing number of Indigenous artists whose work is worthy of study. And unfortunately, most book-length studies of Indigenous literatures do not include chapters devoted to the study of graphic novels. Regrettably, I authored one such recent book; it would have been a better book had I included at least one chapter focusing on the work of a graphic novelist. That oversight is one of many reasons why I wrote this book.[9]

All that said, there is certainly a growing number of scholars turning their attention to the study of Indigenous comics, represented by the rising number of panels at national and international conferences, the publication of articles in journals representing the fields of Indigenous studies and comics studies,[10] and the recent release of one edited collection that productively situates itself in both fields, Frederick Luis Aldama's (2020) *Graphic Indigeneity: Comix in the Americas and Australasia*, which collects essays devoted to the study of Indigenous comics artists producing work in several nations across multiple continents. All of this exciting work signals a major change in literary studies, one in which Indigenous authors are finally being recognized as producers of quality work in popular narrative media and taken seriously by scholars as narrative and visual artists while doing so.

These changes in the academic world—as well as the difficulty Indigenous authors have faced in the popular market—can be explained by the concept of narrative permissibility as developed by Christopher González (2017), who argues, "Certain historically marginalized groups in the United States resist this metaphor of the melting pot because they feel they have not had an opportunity for the same level of self-expression as the dominant group" (1). In his study *Permissible Narratives: The Promise of Latino/a Literature*, González articulates some of the difficulties Latinx writers have faced based on narrow expectations shaped by the publishing industry as well as the larger reading public. What, González asks, is permissible for the Latinx author to write/publish/expect an audience to read (and, by implication, teach and publish research on)? Though focused on Latinx authors, González's work frames the issue for Indigenous authors just as clearly. For instance, González notes that, while it may seem "commonsensical on its face," Latinx authors require "an audience willing to engage with the variety of . . . writing" produced by the artistic community (3). However, that audience is often cultivated by an industry that shapes audience expectations as much as it responds to the desires of the readership (often reflected through sales). And just as "major publishing houses were selective in the Latino/a novels they published" (5), so too have Indigenous authors found that major publishing houses tend to have a rather narrow understanding of "Native American literature."

Akin to how "early successes of Latino/a authors have made it difficult for successive generations of Latino/a writers to write in a manner that differed from those well-established literary tropes" (González 2017, 6), the shape of "Native American literature" has largely been defined by the so-called "Native American Renaissance." Coined by Kenneth Lincoln (1983) in his 1983 study *Native American Renaissance*—and reinforced by countless literary studies and college syllabi—this "movement" has come to define the field of Native American literature (at least in the United States) in the wake of N. Scott Momaday (Kiowa) winning the 1969 Pulitzer Prize for Fiction for his 1968 novel *House Made of Dawn*. Put simply, authors who have come to be associated with this "renaissance" are those whose works engage tribal histories and/or spiritual traditions, express themes associated with cultural and/or political reclamation, and are composed with a stylistic complexity akin to the prevailing postmodernist aesthetic that then dominated the literary canon. In addition to Momaday, authors like Paula Gunn Allen (Laguna Pueblo), Louise Erdrich (Turtle Mountain Chippewa), Leslie Marmon Silko (Laguna Pueblo), James Welch (Blackfeet/A'ainin), and Gerald Vizenor (Anishinaabe), among others, still dominate many syllabi for courses in Native American literature. Of course, I'm not suggesting that these authors should not be widely read and studied; however, following González, I am positing that the well-deserved popular and critical successes enjoyed by these authors have shaped both the market and audience expectations. In particular, the focus on such works has left little room for authors writing in more popular genres. And while we are currently witnessing Indigenous authors beginning to receive acclaim—in the form of publishing deals with major presses, literary awards, and increased attention from scholars—for work in more popular genres, like apocalyptic horror (Cherie Dimaline [Métis]) and fantasy (Daniel Heath Justice [Cherokee]), among others, the larger comics industry has not yet caught on to the wonderful work being produced by Indigenous creators. However, we need to also remember that (as of this writing) we are more than fifty years removed from the publication of *House Made of Dawn* and nearly forty years removed from Lincoln's then-field-defining (albeit problematic) study. While Indigenous artists have continued to publish in a variety of genres and narrative formats—including but not limited to comics and graphic novels—neither the publishing industry nor the academy have yet caught up.

In short, the major publishing houses in comics and graphic novels are not publishing the work of Indigenous creators, and audiences for Indigenous writing who have been shaped by the "Native American Renaissance"—as well as comics audiences who have been shaped by the field dominated by the likes of Marvel, DC, Vertigo, Dark Horse, and others—are not expecting them to do so. If there appears to be no national market yet for such works, this is because the major publishers in the comics industry have neither courted nor crafted it.[11]

• • •

Given their absence from the catalogues of major publishers, Indigenous creators continuing to produce work can be understood as engaging in a political act, asserting themselves against the material realities of the publishing world. This kind of assertion can be read as one form of what author and critic Gerald Vizenor (2009) would consider an act of "survivance," an act that "creates a sense of narrative resistance to absence, literary tragedy, nihility, and victimry." As he continues in his "Introduction" to the collection *Native Liberty*: "Native survivance is an active sense of presence over historical absence, the dominance of cultural simulations, and manifest manners. Native survivance is a continuance of stories" (1). Indigenous comics artists diligently working to produce and distribute their work—from working together on Kickstarter projects, like the *Moonshot* series (discussed in chapter 2), to self-publishing their series[12]—are actively countering their "absence" in the larger comics marketplace, a contemporary as well as a historical absence. Further, by producing such work—and, as we will see in the following chapters, the wide diversity of kinds of work in comics and graphic novels—Indigenous creators are also countering the historical dominance of "simulations" (1), those stereotypical images of Indigenous peoples that have long populated the pages of comic books (and later, graphic novels).[13] Finally, these artists and their works are actively countering what Vizenor terms "manifest manners" (1), a shorthand for the machinery of settler colonialism or the continuation of the long efforts begun by Manifest Destiny. As we will see in the following chapters, in some instances, this means the production of stories that directly engage settler colonialism as a subject, actively countering its rhetoric and imagery; in other instances, this means the production of stories that do not openly address it, providing narratives of Indigenous peoples that are not dependent upon reading them and their art only as a response to Europeans and their descendants. In short, the various narratives of survivance discussed throughout this book provide but a small glimpse of the variety of narratives being produced, all of which collectively reject the central effort of settler colonialism: the erasure of Indigenous peoples and their cultures from our collective imagination as well as from the physical landscape.

Daniel Heath Justice (2018) made this point about Indigenous literatures more broadly in his academic study *Why Indigenous Literatures Matter*, in which he not only makes the case for the importance of Indigenous literatures (remembering González's points above) but also explains, for non-Indigenous readers, the larger cultural importance of Indigenous literature *for Indigenous peoples*. He makes this case by asking—and exploring in great depth—four key questions (which make up the central chapters of his study): "How Do We Learn to Be Human?," "How Do We Behave as Good Relatives?," "How

Do We Become Good Ancestors?," and "How Do We Learn to Live Together?"[14] These questions are rooted in Indigenous epistemologies rather than responses to settler colonialism. As Justice himself writes, "Indigenous texts are by and large responsive, not reactive." That is to say, while Indigenous artists of course respond to the history and continuation of settler colonialism as part of their lived cultural and material histories, Indigenous literatures are not just a reaction to such histories. Indigenous literatures exist—especially for Indigenous audiences—as "one more vital way that we have countered those forces of erasure and given shape to our own ways of being in the world" (xix). Indigenous literatures—and this includes Indigenous comics—serve the important purpose of promoting the values of Indigenous communities for Indigenous readers but also introducing those values to non-Indigenous readers (particularly those who may only be familiar with the stereotypes developed throughout the long history of American comics).

Writing about African American comics artists, Frances Gateward and John Jennings (2015) assert, "Comix traffic in stereotypes and fixity. It is one of the attributes at the heart of how the medium deals with representation" (2). Artists from populations that have historically been limited to stereotypical representations—such as Indigenous, African American, and Latinx populations, among many others—often work to correct such efforts on behalf of the larger comics industry. As a visual as well as a textual medium, comics are able to portray Indigenous peoples—as well as objects, ceremonies, and practices, and epistemologically different representations of concepts, such as time—in ways that purely verbal texts cannot. As such, comics can provide more information, more data, allowing for a more honest characterization that may be lost to readers who have no visual reference or whose visual references have been developed by the stereotypes and misinformation that have been promoted by the comics industry to date.

That said, issues of representation can also become central when non-Indigenous artists are working on texts that are otherwise designated as "Indigenous authored"; this is a particularly important issue with respect to comics, which are often (but not always) produced by a team of artists working together. In some cases—such as the works produced by Tso and Michael Nicoll Yahgulanaas (Haida)—one artist produces the entire work. In many other cases, however—as is the case for the majority of works discussed in the following chapters— the work is written by one artist, with other artists providing the illustrations, coloring, lettering, etc. One such example is the work of writer David Alexander Robertson (Norway House Cree) and his long-time collaborator Scott B. Henderson, who has also worked with other Indigenous writers, including Katherena Vermette (Métis) and Van Camp. Given that comics are a visual art form—and much of the analysis in the following chapters will focus on the visual artistry of the narratives—it might seem problematic to attribute this work to an Indigenous author, effectively erasing the illustrator. Following the general conventions of the field, the writer will be treated as the primary "artist" behind the work. When appropriate, the illustra- tor will be noted. That said, there will be a few instances in which the object of analysis is produced by a non-Indigenous illustrator. In all cases, we should remember the importance of collaborative, community-based work in Indigenous communities, including artis- tic communities. The non-Indigenous artists contributing to such books are collaborating with Indigenous authors to tell stories impor- tant to Indigenous communities. At no point will I be designating the works themselves as "Indigenous," nor will I be adopting a ver- sion of "blood-quantum" thinking to determine if there are enough Indigenous artists working on a project. Each work discussed in the chapters below is written by an Indigenous author, and some of those authors have chosen to work with non-Indigenous collaborators to help bring their artistic visions to completion. In this regard, the collaboratively produced works discussed in the chapters that follow practice an artistic version of Justice's (2018) answer to the question "How Do We Learn to Live Together?": "Finding common ground that honours justice, embraces the truths of our shared history, and works for better futures" (179).

• • •

As we will see in the chapters below, many Indigenous comics art- ists frame their works within well-known genres—such as science fiction and superhero comics—in order to challenge genre-based tropes and promote a socio-political agenda, while others compose experimentally in order to craft new narrative opportunities to engage in that same kind of work. So, while there are a multitude of ways of organizing and analyzing the wide diversity of comics that have thus far been produced—some of which I will allude to in the coda—I have chosen to organize my chapters here by genre, in part because of genre's framework for organizing information and providing a useful analytical lens.

In a statement that could apply to a great many areas of literary theory, David Duff (2000)—in his introduction to the collection *Modern Genre Theory*—notes that "few concepts have proved more problematic and unstable than that of genre" (1). And while this claim has been borne out in conferences as well as in print, academics are not alone in their arguments. Fans of any genre of film, music, and television have long engaged in debates about the scope of a particular genre and what texts do or do not belong: is *The Silence of the Lambs* horror or thriller?[15] Is Black Sabbath heavy metal or hard rock? Is *Firefly* sci-fi just because it takes place in outer space, or is it better understood as a western, set in outer space? These questions become more interesting—and perhaps even more difficult to answer—when we begin considering art and artists that consciously blend recognizable genres and bend or even break the expectations of those genres.

However interesting such discussions may be, they tend to rest on the assumption that genre is a little more than a checklist, with genre-based determinations based on how many boxes a particular text (or artist) checks off. Further, even in those instances of which the two sides of the debate cannot agree on the nature of the checklist—for example, whether a movie has to include jump scares and gore to be considered a horror film—the underlying premise still seems to be that genre is little more than a means of categorization. As John Frow (2006) argues in his study *Genre*, however, genre is better understood as a method of interpretation. Frow writes:

> Genre, we might say, is a set of conventional and highly organized constraints on the production of meaning. In using the word "constraint" I don't mean to say that genre is simply

a restriction. Rather, its structuring effects are productive of meaning; they shape and guide, in the way that a builder's form gives shape to a pour of concrete, or a sculptor's mold shapes and gives structure to its materials. (10)

Far from ignoring the "checklist" approach, Frow recognizes that such checklists provide a foundation for understanding how texts generate meaning. When a reader (or audience member) recognizes the conventions of a genre, they begin to understand how to interpret that text, how the various pieces—the overall structure, the tropes employed, etc.—build meaning based on their previous usage in related texts. This is because, "like formal structures generally, [genre] works at a level of semiosis—that is, of meaning-making—which is deeper and more forceful than the explicit 'content' of a text" (Frow 2006, 19). What the text is "about," in other words, is far less important than the means by which the text is constructed. And in some cases, readers already begin to construct the meaning of the text from such paratextual materials as the title and cover art, as well as placement in bookstores or advertising algorithms designed by online booksellers, like Amazon.[16]

Frow (2006) takes the performative meaning making of genre one step further when he claims, "far from being merely 'stylistic' devices, genres create effects of reality and truth which are central to the different ways the world is understood" (19). Put simply, genre can determine how we see not just the texts that we read but also the world in which we live. Just as the genre of the western has largely whitewashed America's past, thus giving rise to a mistaken belief in the ubiquity of white (that is, non-Indigenous and non-Latinx) people and cultural norms often referenced by white supremacists to support their exclusionary national identity, and just as romantic comedies often normalize heterosexual relationships (as well as very specific rules of courtship and relationship goals) in such a way that defines queer sexual couplings as socially undesirable, all genres (to some degree) work to shape the reality of their audiences. How we understand the world in which we live, in other words, is shaped by the genre conventions of the stories that we tell. In short, "genres are facts of culture" (53).

As Mark C. Jerng (2018) demonstrates in his study *Racial World-making: The Power of Popular Fiction*, one of those "facts of culture" is race, a cultural "fact" that popular genres have helped to establish and disseminate to reading audiences for generations. Studying such popular genres as the plantation romance, sword-and-sorcery fantasy, and alternate histories (though his arguments are certainly not limited to these genres alone), Jerng argues that "these genre fictions are the center of what I call *racial worldmaking*," which is what he terms "narrative and interpretive strategies that shape how readers notice race so as to build, anticipate, and organize the world" (1–2; emphasis original). Rather than focusing on the "visual epistemology of race"— that is, what we see when we see race—Jerng's study explores the "*salience of race*," or the means by which "we are taught when, where, and how race is something to notice" (2; emphasis original). Calling back Frow's language as well as his premise, Jerng notes that "genre helps us consider more closely how sequences are interpreted, how contexts are generated, and how statements gain exploratory force"; among those sequences and contexts, of course, is race. And "because we *participate in genres* in order to form and organize our sense of the world" (9; emphasis original), such participation helps us form and organize our understanding of race. Recognizing this, one way Indigenous comics artists are consciously participating in this "worldmaking"—this process of shaping how their readers understand the world in which they live—is by writing in and actively reshaping various genres familiar to their audiences. As such, the texts discussed in the chapters below can be said to be engaging with genres in order to further the potential of "antiracist worldmaking" (217) that Jerng calls for at the end of his study.[17]

Once we recognize the importance of genre more generally, we can begin considering the importance of the specific genres discussed below. Of course, one major reason for the genres selected below is their popularity among Indigenous artists, reflecting (in part) the popularity of these genres more generally. There is no shortage of science fiction or superhero comics, for instance, and I have no doubt that several more will be published while this book is readied for publication. But more importantly, each of the genres discussed below carry significant cultural importance that is often not associated with

Indigenous populations.[18] Science fiction narratives, for instance, are expressions of a technologically advanced future that almost always imagines that future without Indigenous peoples and cultures. As such, writing themselves into that genre inserts Indigenous peoples into a cultural space from which they have been quietly excluded; this is an act of political survivance. Similarly, superhero comics have often been used to bolster nationalistic claims based on physical force and the attendant belief that some people are more powerful (and therefore more deserving) than others. The lack of Indigenous super-heroes—or, more importantly, the lack of Indigenous superheroes not drawn from stereotypes—could thus be read as a comment about the collective national vision of Indigenous participation in the body politic as well as a reminder that Indigenous peoples are not seen as strong, national leaders who can embody "America." There is a similar issue with respect to historical narratives, given the white-washing of America's history and the replacing of Indigenous peoples and cultures with stereotypes, which run from the inaccurate to the hurtful. Finally, a chapter on experimental narratives highlights the importance of recognizing continuing contributions by Indigenous artists to new aesthetic (formal and stylistic) developments while alluding to the political possibilities of formal narrative and aesthetic experimentation.

In chapter 1, "Super Problems Require Super Heroes: Indigenous Superheroes and Their Communities," I provide an analysis of many of the superhero comics that have been produced by Indigenous artists in the United States and Canada. Stories of caped crusaders and heroes with enhanced powers have long been part of the comics industry, and their popularity has only increased with the unprec-edented success of such movie/TV franchises as the Marvel Cinematic Universe. Having long been written out of this popular tradition—either through their absence or through inaccurate representation by the use of stereotypes—Indigenous creators are inserting Indigenous heroes into the larger superhero landscape. More importantly, these comics engage this genre in order to perform narrative activism, drawing attention to and combating many of the social and political ills facing Indigenous peoples today, against which many of these superheroes fight.

Chapter 2, "Indigenous Travels in Space, Time, and Technology," explores a sampling of the science fiction narratives composed by Indigenous creators. Although science fiction narratives have often included either implicit or explicit references to Indigenous peoples (or the concept of "Indigeneity" more broadly), as with superhero comics, these references have often been rooted in stereotypes or drawn from the settler-colonial ideology that identifies Indigenous peoples as belonging to an uncivilized past. Rooted in the larger contemporary movement of Indigenous futurism, Indigenous creators turn this history on its head by crafting narratives of exploration and discovery that place Indigenous people as the adventurers, as leaders of a technological future instead of relics of pretechnological history. And in doing so, these narratives engage issues facing Indigenous peoples and suggest potential solutions.

Chapter 3, "The Past Is Part of the Present: Indigenous Historical Graphic Narratives," examines in depth two ongoing series by Indigenous creators that explore important moments and peoples from First Nations, Métis, and Inuit (Canadian) history. Specifically, these series use a variety of narrative aesthetic devices to explicitly connect the present to the past, thus providing a subtle but powerful argument about the ongoing importance of understanding the past for contemporary Indigenous peoples. In ways not wholly dissimilar to the previous chapter, this chapter explicitly disavows the continuation of the ideology that Indigeneity is fixed in the past; rather, in the comics selected, the past and the present are inextricably woven together in ways that also, at times, reflect an understanding of time that counters the modern Western view of time as a strict linear chronology.

Finally, in chapter 4, "Pushing the Boundaries of Representation: Indigenous Experimental Graphic Narrative," I highlight the work of two graphic novelists whose work engages with formal experimentation with respect to the traditional narrative formatting, sequencing, or aesthetics most often found in graphic narratives. Often not associated with the literary avant-garde, many Indigenous creators blend traditional tribal arts with new technological advances and creative mashups of various cultural artistic practices. In addition to exploring new directions for the larger artistic form, these formal experimentations also provide new means of drawing attention to and confronting the continued absence of Indigenous peoples and cultures while inviting readers into new ways of approaching and understanding Indigenous peoples and their cultural projects.

• • •

Hopefully, these few pages have already answered the first question posed in this introduction's title: Why Indigenous comics? The second question—why now?—I have only hinted at. As this book demonstrates, there is a large and growing number of artists producing compelling and important work. (In the coda, I will gesture toward additional means of understanding and analyzing these texts.) This is an exciting time for Indigenous comics artists and, as such, an exciting time for readers of comics. Working within popular genres that appeal to a broad range of readers, the Indigenous authors discussed in the chapters below will no doubt appeal to such readers. Indigenous comics artists should be more popular than they are and are more than deserving of the readership, awards, and other accolades enjoyed by their non-Indigenous contemporaries.

However, the primary audience for this particular book is academic. And more academics should be turning their attention to these creators, as well as the many others producing such work. Although recent scholarship reflects the growing interest in this work, comics scholars have long ignored the work of Indigenous artists, while scholars in Indigenous studies have not yet turned their full attention to this work either. Now is the time. There is a great deal of interesting, exciting, aesthetically appealing, and politically compelling work waiting for academic as well as popular audiences to take note. These works should be on the shelves of bookstores, listed on course syllabi, and, most importantly, in the hands of the many readers who no doubt would enjoy them.

It's time for readers of all stripes to catch up to the wonderful work being done by Indigenous comics artists.

SUPER PROBLEMS REQUIRE SUPER HEROES

Indigenous Superheroes and Their Communities

Metropolis, Gotham City, Wakanda, Atlantis, Themyscira, Vegas Valley Paiute Reservation, Leaning Oak Reservation. These fictional locations are synonymous with the heroes that defend them: Superman, Batman, Black Panther, Aquaman, Wonder Woman, Captain Paiute, Super Indian.

The latter two superheroes are not household names whose presence in a blockbuster movie guarantee commercial success. (At least not yet.[1]) Rather, they are but two of the relatively new Indigenous-created Native American superheroes whose current series are both participating in as well as critiquing the superhero tradition in mainstream American comics. Possessing powers that manifested after accidents, secret identities that help protect their loved ones from being targeted, colorful spandex costumes, and an unshakeable moral code insisting that the innocent must be protected from those who would do them harm, Captain Paiute and Super Indian are in one respect Indigenous versions of traditional Marvel- and DC-style comic-book superheroes.[2] However, unlike their mainstream world-beater counterparts, they are not engaged in defending the planet from intergalactic threats, like Doomsday, Darkseid, or Ares, or even human antagonists, like Lex Luthor and the Joker, whose efforts are directed toward world domination or destructive chaos. Rather, these superheroes focus their attention on their immediate communities: reservations and tribal communities. With their ongoing hero series, Native American creators Theo Tso (Las Vegas Paiute) and Arigon Starr (Kickapoo) are using the genre of the "superhero comic" to productively engage in tribal politics, raising awareness about just a few of the social and political injustices faced by contemporary Indigenous peoples and their reservation communities. And as we see in the works of other comics artists such as Jay Odjick (Anishinabe), Jon Proudstar (Yaqui), Stephen Graham Jones (Blackfeet), and Gord Hill (Kwakwaka'wakw), superhero comics also provide a space for myriad kinds of creative intervention and political commentary.

While the genre of the "superhero comic" may engage a large number of Indigenous participants in works potentially appealing to the largest possible readership—given the continued popularity of superhero comics, especially in a pop culture universe dominated by the Marvel Cinematic Universe—many of the titles I will discuss below are hard to find and/or out of print. Creators like Tso and Starr have self-published their works; while Starr's books can be ordered online by such third-party sellers as Amazon, Tso's works are not nationally distributed (I ordered my copies directly from Tso himself via Facebook). Despite their potential for success in a market that is eagerly consuming narratives following the adventures of masked heroes, Indigenous superheroes remain largely unknown to the general readership. Much of this can be attributed to the publishing industry itself, which has historically ignored much of Indigenous literary production before the so-called "Native American Renaissance" (roughly 1968–1997) and even much of the work following that period that did not fit the mold of what became expected for Indigenous writers: a reclamation of traditional tribal culture, particularly as it manifested in the lives of contemporary Indigenous peoples, in literary fiction. Speculative fiction by Indigenous writers in particular has largely been ignored. For instance, while James Welch (Blackfeet/A'ainin) and Leslie Marmon Silko (Laguna Pueblo) continue to receive much (well-deserved) attention for their award-winning novels that engage tribal history and culture, their contemporary Misha (Métis) has seen her remarkable 1990 steampunk novel *Red Spider White Web* go out of print twice. And while I am likely reducing a complex situation down to an overly simplistic claim, we cannot ignore the importance of the publishing industry on creating the very market it serves. In his study of Latino/a authors and the publishing industry, *Permissible Narratives*, Christopher González (2017) notes the constraints placed on Latino/a writers generally and comics artists specifically, who are often held by publishers to "identity-based expectations" (109).[3] And works that do not fit into the mold approved of by focus groups, popular readers, and the publishing industry that shapes them, may be doomed to become what González calls "lost texts" (12). In a world where the vast majority of superheroes in Western popular culture are white, Indigenous superheroes simply do not fit. And Indigenous comics creators have yet to receive the attention and recognition as their peers who compose "literary fiction." In two senses, Indigenous comics creators are producing "lost texts" well worthy of discovery.

Thus, the popularity of superhero comics may be as much a curse as a blessing, for while the genre remains commercially successful and open to an increasingly large cast of heroes, the large number of texts may also (albeit unwittingly at times) solidify audience expectations and standardize norms for the heroes.[4] For instance, the Marvel Cinematic Universe is largely white, with no acknowledgement of Indigenous peoples. Just as Consuela Francis (2015) notes that "black readers long for black superheroes" (141), so too do Indigenous readers long for Indigenous superheroes. And as we will see below, those heroes exist and are well worth reading about. Frederick Luis Aldama (2017) takes this point one step further; he notes that Latinx readers of superhero comics are waiting for "DC and Marvel [to] come see [them] as potential readers and, therefore, as potential *buyers* of comics" (90). Indigenous superheroes, for all that they conform to the standards of the genre (as we will see below), may not be appealing to publishers or the market those publishers wish to serve, even if those comics check all the appropriate boxes. That said, Indigenous comics creators are also consciously subverting certain key aspects of the superhero genre. While on the one hand, such acts of subversion can be read as groundbreaking or innovative, on the other hand, such moves can potentially distance an audience. For instance, as Scott Bukatman (2013) notes in his essay "A Song of the Urban Superhero," "superheroes, many of whom could, let's face it, live anywhere they want, invariably reside in American cities" (170). Many publishers (and readers) may then dismiss the potential of Indigenous superheroes who live on reservations and exclusively serve tribal communities, mistakenly assuming that such works only appeal to a niche audience.

Similarly, for all that the academic community has trumpeted the importance of diversity in the study of superhero comics (and comics more generally), Indigenous superheroes are often left out of that discussion. To give but one paradigmatic example, in their chapter on "Diversity in Superheroes" in their study *Enter the Superheroes*, Alex S. Romagnoli and Gian S. Pagnucci (2013) make no mention of Indigenous superheroes and limit their discussion to two case studies: "Miles Morales, a half-black and half-Hispanic teenager" and "the hypersexualized depiction of Starfire and Catwoman in DC's New 52 reboot" (134). Similarly, in his contribution to *The Cambridge History of the Graphic Novel*, Darren Harris-Fain (2018) writes:

> It is worth noting that, like such examples of the literary canon, most writers of superhero graphic novels, like most readers, have been straight, white, and male. Occasionally the work of a woman or a writer of color, as with Gail Simone or Jodi Picoult on *Wonder Woman* or Ta-Nehisi Coates on *Black Panther*, makes headlines, but sadly this is in part because of the rarity of female or minority writers in superhero graphic novels. (507)

While this point is certainly worth making, Harris-Fain does little to address the issue in his chapter. There is no shortage of women and nonwhite artists writing superhero graphic novels, and that number gets larger when we accept that many "superhero graphic novels" are bound editions of collected works that were originally printed serially. Not only does he include very few examples of such writers in his chapter, but not one of them is an Indigenous creator. However, he is correct when he notes that these writers do not make headlines; that said, the only way to counter this is to then write those headlines, making Indigenous creators central to our discussion of the genre.

With the remainder of this chapter, then, I would like to insert Indigenous superheroes into the academic discussion, just as Indigenous creators have inserted Indigenous superheroes into the genre, demonstrating how such superheroes fit the traditional mold of the American comic-book superhero while simultaneously revising the genre for explicitly political ends. This chapter will open with an analysis of Las Vegas Paiute author Theo Tso's and Kickapoo artist Arigon

Starr's ongoing series *Captain Paiute* and *Super Indian*. I will follow this discussion with an analysis of one-off titles by Kitigan Zibi Anishinabe artist Jay Odjick (*Kagagi*), Yaqui artist Jon Proudstar (*Tribal Force*), and Blackfeet writer Stephen Graham Jones (*My Hero*) before analyzing the use of superhero comic artistry in the political work of Kwakwaka'wakw artist/activist Gord Hill's *The Antifa Comic Book*.

• • •

In his article "The Definition of the Superhero," Peter Coogan (2009) outlines the various criteria that define the figure of the comic-book superhero. Building off of Judge Learned Hand's 1952 copyright ruling finding "that Wonder Man copied and infringed upon Superman" as well as noting that both Wonder Man and Superman were "'champion[s] of the oppressed' who combat 'evil and injustice,'" Coogan identifies "the mission convention" as "essential to the superhero genre." Put simply, "someone who does not act selflessly to aid others in times of need is not heroic and therefore not a hero" (77). However, selfless acts of heroism are not enough to identify a character as a "superhero" in the comics tradition (even if Arigon Starr will potentially challenge this idea in her works, as we will see below). Additionally, traditional comic-book superheroes must possess some kind of power, given that "superpowers are the most identifiable elements of the superhero genre" (78). And though it should go without saying, use of these powers must be limited to selfless acts of heroism; the Flash does not participate in track meets. Nor, of course, could Barry Allen do so without sacrificing his "secret identity," the final piece of the "three elements—mission, powers, and identity, or MPI—[that] establish the core of the genre" (82). As we will see below, both Captain Paiute and Super Indian possess the MPI matrix that recognizably identifies the comic-book superhero.

Comic-book superheroes also often employ a costume, which serves multiple purposes. Most importantly, it separates the heroic identity from the secret identity, allowing the two to remain individual personae (perhaps most famously in the split between the charming and self-confident Superman vs. the bumbling and socially inept Clark Kent). As Coogan (2009) notes, "the identity element comprises the

codename and the costume, with the secret identity being a custom-
ary counterpart to the codename" (78). By noting it as a codename,
Coogan is suggesting that the "secret identity" is the "true identity,"
while the superhero identity is a role or a performance. We see this in
the way that multiple individuals can assume the mantle of a superhero identity—and all wear similar versions of the costume—such as
when John Stewart replaced Guy Gardner as Hal Jordan's backup in
the Green Lantern Corps or the way Peter Parker, Miles Morales, and
Miguel O'Hara all simultaneously operate as Spider-Man in different narrative arcs. The costume, along with the codename, also does
more than simply name the superhero; for Superman, "his codename
expresses his character," whereas for Batman, "his codename embodies
his biography." Similarly, Superman's use of bright primary colors not
only marks him visually but also suggests his straightforward moral
code, whereas Batman's dark costume—useful for prowling the city at
night—reminds readers of his questionable moral character, not being
above extreme acts of violence and even torture to achieve his ends.
Superheroes also tend to—but need not always—possess some sort of
emblem on their costume that operates as a visual shorthand: Superman's S and Batman's bat chest piece have become common symbols
in American popular culture and serve as "iconic representations of
the superhero identity" (79).[5] Often, but again not always, these costumes employ some sort of mask, protecting the superhero's secret
identity (and thus, in theory if not in practice, protecting the hero's
loved ones from becoming targets for revenge). Clark Kent's glasses
serve the same purpose, if in a reverse fashion, and some heroes, like
Wonder Woman, wear no mask at all.[6]

Of course, as with all literary genres, these distinctions are fluid
by nature and can be present to greater or lesser degrees without
the risk of a character losing his/her superhero status. For instance,
the Fantastic Four may have used codenames, but their nonheroic
identities were never kept secret from the public. Luke Cage may
have briefly gone by the moniker Power Man, but even early on, that
nickname was secondary to his given name. And the Black Panther
is always the King of Wakanda. Similarly, there are various narrative
conventions that are employed by superhero comic-book story arcs,
such as the articulation of an origin story for the superhero's powers

(which often is also directly tied to the character's motivations for hero work), as well as continuity within the shared universe populated by other superheroes. As we will see below, both Super Indian and Captain Paiute possess origin stories that explain their powers and clearly tie their missions to local reservation politics. However, neither hero exists in the same "universe" as other superheroes; in fact, one of their functions is to remind readers that mainstream superheroes have never been concerned with reservation populations or their specific needs. This lack of connection to a larger narrative universe, however, should not be read as a deficiency. Not only is such a larger "universe" not possible with relatively new books from independent presses, but such participation would also work counter to the political aims of the two series. Where the various superheroes in the ever-expanding Marvel Cinematic Universe are largely engaged in international and even intergalactic warfare, protecting the United States specifically and planet Earth more generally from villains bent on domination, Captain Paiute and Super Indian are hyperfocused on protecting their immediate reservation communities from real-world threats.[7]

As *Captain Paiute* and *Super Indian* demonstrate, Indigenous populations continue to face a variety of threats—physical threats, political threats, and the ever-increasing pressure to abandon their cultural heritage and assimilate into Euro-American culture—and the Indigenous superheroes are used to confront such threats directly. Employing the "MPI matrix" that Coogan articulates, Indigenous comic artists are constructing superheroes that draw from mainstream superhero comics in order to attend to the continued threats to Indigenous peoples living in reservation communities. Additionally, such heroes as Super Indian and Captain Paiute counter what Chris Gavaler (2018) identifies as the "superhero's imperial roots." For Gavaler, the "imperial superhero" is a manifestation of an empire's claim as a rightfully dominating power over global possessions," and as such, "contemporary superhero comics remain haunted by that imperial past" (34). For obvious reasons, Indigenous superheroes break that mold, particularly by resisting the efforts of imperialization/colonization still engaged by the United States and Canada against tribal populations. Indigenous superheroes similarly do not fall into Gavaler's identification of "the wellborn superhero," characterized as "millionaire playboy by

day, crime-fighting do-gooder by night" (49)—think of Batman or the
Green Arrow—particularly because these superheroes are reservation born and live lives "by day" facing all the socio-economic issues
involved in reservation life (which for many includes poverty). In this
regard, Indigenous superheroes can be read as charting out a new tra-
jectory for superhero comics more generally while still employing the
foundational traits of the genre. In short, Indigenous superheroes are
not just traditional superheroes played by Indigenous actors; rather,
they are reimaginations of the figure of the superhero, constructed to
explicitly combat threats that mainstream superheroes—much like
mainstream society—have ignored.

• • •

Employing a visual aesthetic (especially in the cover art) and narrative form reminiscent of Bronze Age comic storytelling (roughly
1970–1985), Theo Tso's *Captain Paiute* follows the adventures of Luther
Pah, mild-mannered tribal hydrologist by profession who, chosen by
the Paiute water spirit Pah, was granted control over water (employing
everything from mist to ice darts and the ability to harden his skin,
giving him super strength, depending on the situation). Engaging
contemporary politics immediately with this series, the first page[8]
of issue 1 (Tso 2017a, n.p. 1; figure 1.1) shows Captain Paiute in his
costume proudly standing in front of the residents of the Vegas
Valley Paiute Reservation (a barely fictionalized version of the Las
Vegas Indian Colony reservation), many of whom are holding signs
opposing some of the most devastating political pressures currently
facing Indigenous reservations in North America: one sign reads
"#NoDAPL" (referring to the Dakota Access Pipeline), another reads
"OIL = DEATH" (referencing the various times Indigenous populations have been relocated when their lands were discovered to sit atop
oil reserves), and the final sign proclaims "IDLE NO MORE!" (referring to the grassroots protest movement started in 2012 in Canada
originally founded to oppose Bill C-45[9]). This opening page is not
situated in the story that follows but rather serves as a visual introduction to the superhero and his mission.

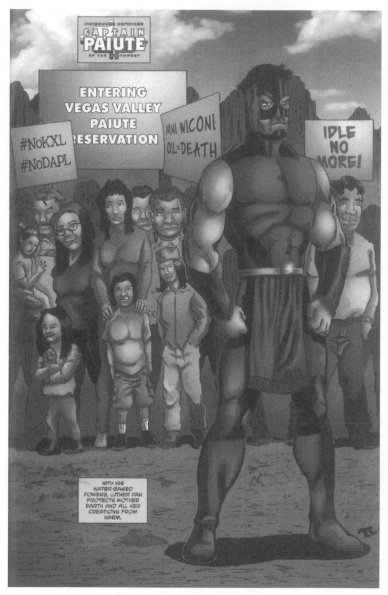

Figure 1.1. Theo Tso, *Captain Paiute*, vol. 1.

With the first page of the first full issue of the series, Theo Tso boldly presents the reader with a visual rendition of Captain Paiute's "MPI matrix"—mission, powers, and identity—as a means of introducing the narrative that follows. Standing in the foreground we have Captain Paiute himself, dressed in a blue spandex suit and mask with a red loin cloth and yellow belt, wearing the primary colors that have adorned many mainstream superheroes. Chest out, eyes fixed determinedly ahead, Captain Paiute is clearly protecting the reservation inhabitants who are actively protesting some of the various abuses currently being borne by Indigenous populations in North America; as such, Captain Paiute's mission is clearly identified as both protector of his reservation community as well as symbol for the protection of Indigenous rights more broadly. And in a text box at the bottom of the page, Captain Paiute is identified as Luther Pah, whose name alludes to the water spirit who granted him his powers. Captain Paiute's MPI matrix thus serves to clearly identify him as a superhero with strong ties to his reservation community and tribal heritage. And given the loosely fictionalized version of the Vegas Valley Paiute Indians—and especially the real-life concerns they are protesting on the opening page—*Captain Paiute* is also meant to serve as a call to arms for contemporary Indigenous communities standing against myriad real-world problems.

In addition to the MPI matrix that clearly identifies him as a superhero, in this first issue, the reader is introduced to Captain Paiute's "origin story," an explanation as to how he acquired his powers and identified his mission. With most comic-book superheroes, the powers are acquired first, and the mission is identified later, such as when Peter Parker develops his powers after being bitten by a radioactive spider; Parker first uses those powers for financial gain (as a professional fighter) before the murder of his Uncle Ben—murdered at the hands of a criminal Parker chose not to stop—directed him to a life of heroism. In the case of *Captain Paiute*, Luther Pah understands immediately Spider-Man's dictum that "with great power comes great responsibility"; in fact, such an understanding is one reason why he was chosen. Drawing his power from the water spirit, Captain Paiute must, from time to time, replenish those powers by immersing himself into water. In one such trip, we are presented with a flashback explaining his origin: after accidentally falling through a crevice while hiking, Luther Pah nearly died of hypothermia before the water spirit manifested to choose Luther as his champion, telling him: "Water is life. You are the chosen one. Defender of the land. Protector of the people" (Tso 2017a, n.p. 16). After accidentally spilling sulfuric acid on himself and instinctively flushing it out with the water stored in his body, Pah then began experimenting with his powers and stopping local crime before formally adopting the mantle of Captain Paiute. The short issue o that first introduced Captain Paiute has a slightly more detailed version of the origin story: we learn that Pah was the sole survivor of a car crash that took his parents' lives (ominously noting that "someone had plans for me after all"; Tso 2015, n.p. 4) and that he is only the most recent hero chosen by Pah to serve as protector of the Paiute. Explained in the context of the history of the Paiute's oppression at the hands of European colonizers—their forced removal from tribal lands onto reservations and the various abuses of children at boarding schools, including the use of water to violently try to scrub the color off of the skins of Indigenous children—Captain Paiute's origin story is directly tied to his tribal history and traditional beliefs.

Captain Paiute's first enemy is not an otherworldly foe or even a villain from outside the reservation. Rather, his first enemy is Waylon Williams, former resident of the reservation before his family was kicked off for undisclosed "dark and terrible things. Things no one should speak of" (Tso 2017a, n.p. 7). Embodying the common trope of the "evil former friend" long employed by comics writers,[10] Waylon returns to the reservation in the guise of a ground radar specialist in order to gain access to the tribal cemetery. Somehow drawing his powers from his buried ancestors, Waylon—who adopts the name Bad Medicine, whose powers include draining people of their souls and using them to power energy blasts—immediately attacks the reservation residents out of rage for having been (rightfully) banished from the community. While Captain Paiute is off recovering his powers (and giving the reader a chance to read his origin story), Bad Medicine continues to torment the reservation by spreading his "bad medicine" to unleash the residents' rage upon one another. One example of this violence has a tribal police officer about to beat a Black Lives Matter protester while yelling "love it or leave it, Libturd!" (Tso 2019, n.p. 23),

Figure 1.2. Theo Tso, *Captain Paiute*, vol. 1

alluding to nontribal-based political activism and situating the comic squarely in support of another contemporary civil rights movement (figure 1.2).[11] The size and location of the hands holding the Black Lives Matter card—and the angle appearing to look up to the angry officer—both place the reader in the position of the protester, suggesting that the reader of this comic is among those who support such civil rights efforts while also subtly suggesting that the reader could be in danger for doing so. The positioning thus invites the reader into the work of civil rights protesting generally, which certainly includes the work of water protectors as seen in figure 1.1.

My copy of the first issue of *Captain Paiute* (which I ordered from the author directly from his War Paint Studios, whose webpage is—as of this writing—offline and under construction) came with a short comic insert titled "Why an Indigenous Superhero Is Needed?" A reservation resident asks the tribal council to weigh in on the need for Captain Paiute and asks if he poses a threat, especially if "the government gets wind of him and sends in the military" (Tso 2017b, n.p. 1), a not too unreasonable fear given the US government's historically abusive treatment of Indigenous peoples. The council replies that Captain Paiute is necessary to protect the people and their "sacred traditions," adding that murder, rape, and suicide rates have risen across the country among reservation populations. The first council member ends by noting that no other superheroes "have stepped foot on a reservation before," reminding the reader of the large oversight by the mainstream comics industry. Before adjourning the meeting, however, another council member points out that, should the army come, "it wouldn't be the first time that the government has sent soldiers to our reservations . . . nor will it be the last time" (n.p. 1). Read in the context of the story that this insert accompanied, Tso suggests that the various problems faced by the Native American and First Nations reservation communities—problems brought to them by the US and Canadian governments, often with the support of military force—are an ongoing concern for Indigenous populations. As such, superheroes like Captain Paiute are needed, as defenders in fictional narratives as well as sources of inspiration for the current generation of Indigenous activists who will stand up for their lands and their rights, as represented on the first page of the comic.

• • •

Consciously—and even at times satirically—playing with the traditional aspects of the mainstream superhero, Arigon Starr's *Super Indian*[12] also provides a pointed articulation of the various problems inherent in contemporary reservation life. Set on the fictional Leaning Oak Reservation, *Super Indian* follows the heroic acts of Hubert Logan, janitor at the reservation bingo hall, as well as his heroic exploits as Super Indian. Starr's focus on the reservation community is evident from the first pages, which present a cast of characters, including the heroes—Logan/Super Indian, his sidekick, General Bear/Mega Bear (who possesses no powers, but does employ a secret identity), and Logan's talking dog, Diogi—the villains for the volume ("The Circle of Evil"), and twenty of the Leaning Oak residents (including Logan's family[13]), many of whom appear briefly in minor roles (Starr 2012). In short, while Hubert Logan/Super Indian is the eponymous hero, the series' true focus is the Leaning Oak Reservation as a whole and the community that Logan protects.

Super Indian's characterization as a superhero falls squarely into Coogan's "MPI matrix," possessing a clearly defined mission, explicit powers, and a heroic identity separate from his given name. And like many comic-book superheroes, all three are intertwined. Although Super Indian's origin story has not (yet) been narrated in detail, we learn from his character biography that he gained his powers after eating "commodity cheese tainted with 'Rezium,' an experimental element developed by Government Research Scientist Dr. Eaton Crowe to solve world hunger and win the Nobel Prize" (Starr 2012, n.p. iv). We see Starr's pointed sarcasm both in the name of the element— "Rezium," suggesting this element was only included in food sent to reservations—as well as the doctor's name: "eating crow" is an expression used to suggest humiliation after having been proven wrong. That said, Dr. Crowe also won a Nobel Prize, reminding the readers of the long history of white academics flourishing while using Indigenous peoples as experimental (and at times unknowing) test subjects. While Dr. Crowe is a Nobel Prize winner, Hubert Logan remains a janitor. However, the tainted cheese did provide Logan with his powers and can be read as an accident not unlike those that granted powers to such mainstream superheroes as Daredevil and the Incredible Hulk. Although the full extent of his powers is still unknown, Super Indian has employed a "supersonic punch" in addition to super hearing, super strength, and the power of flight. Additionally, Logan consumed this cheese at a birthday party for the "local bully," Derek Thunder, who, possessing a different set of powers, would grow up to become the villain controlling Technoskin, a giant robot who attempts to turn the population of Leaning Oak into zombies by stripping them of their reservation accoutrements (figure 1.3): "Gone are the ribbon

Figure 1.3. Arigon Starr, *Super Indian*, vol. 1.

shirts. The reservation mullets. . . . Conformity *good*. Native culture
bad" (n.p. 45). We see here the villainous nature of Derek Thunder
manifesting as a desire to eliminate individualism as well as some of
the popular forms of personal expression on the reservation, thus
operating as yet another arm of the settler-colonial impulse to force
Indigenous people to conform to standards not of their own design.

As with *Captain Paiute*, one of *Super Indian*'s first villains is a
former but now disgraced member of the reservation community.
And here we see Super Indian's mission: protection of the reservation
community and his community's way of life. In addition to protecting that community from internal threats, like Derek Thunder, and
his efforts at impressing into service an "ambiguously brown army"
(Starr 2012, n.p. 46) to serve as cannon fodder for his evil plans, Super
Indian also protects the reservation from outside threats, many of
which are thinly veiled constructions referencing the ongoing acts of
colonization faced by tribal communities. For instance, Super Indian's
very first antagonist is "the Anthro," "noted German Anthropologist

Professor Karl Von Kelheim" (n.p. 1), who after discovering magic crystals on the Leaning Oak Reservation grew to a giant and terrorized the reservation. Like many anthropologists in the past have done with Indigenous peoples, Dr. Von Kelheim literally put Super Indian under glass, trapping him under a giant specimen jar, while attempting to transform local resident Tillie Thunder into his "giant Native bride" (n.p. 2; figure 1.4). The unnatural coloring of the Anthro's eyes suggest the evil nature of his actions, and the relative sizes of him and Super Indian suggest to the reader the immense power the former has over the latter. Further, this treatment of Super Indian recalls the case of Ishi, known popularly as "the last Yahi" or "the last wild Indian," who lived the remaining years of his life in the Museum of Anthropology at the University of California, Berkeley, where he was studied by the renowned anthropologist Alfred L. Kroeber. Gerald Vizenor (2009), who has written extensively about Ishi, notes, in his chapter "Mr. Ishi of California," that Ishi was "captured," "then sustained as cultural property" while "humanely secured in a museum at a time when natives were denied human and civil rights" (239).[14] Arigon Starr calls to mind not only Ishi and his literal existence "under glass" but all Indigenous peoples who have watched as their cultural traditions have been cheaply adopted by white anthropologists in the name of academic enrichment at the expense of actual Indigenous peoples and their immediate concerns.[15]

Comics historians may read another layer into this representation, however, recalling *Superman* issue 342, "Hero Under Glass!," in which Superman is similarly trapped under glass. Although the story lines are vastly different, the visual of both heroes under glass helps to draw the parallels between Superman, iconic champion of Metropolis, and Super Indian, devoted protector of the Leaning Oak Reservation. Like his near namesake,[16] Super Indian sports a giant red S on his bright blue costume, which is additionally adorned with a belt buckle reading "NDN," common typographic shorthand for "Indian." The clear visual allusion to the Man of Steel connects Super Indian's mission with Superman's—both are self-selected protectors of a people and their way of life—while the belt buckle signals to the reader that Super Indian's mission is focused exclusively on the Indigenous people who previously have not had such a champion. Instead

Figure 1.4. Arigon Starr, *Super Indian*, vol. 1.

of the lofty and abstract goals of "truth, justice, and the American way," Super Indian's efforts are directed to his reservation and their specific needs. For instance, in "The Curse of Blud Kwan'tum" (which takes up most of volume 2; see Starr 2015a), Super Indian saves the reservation from Blud Kwan'tum, descendant of a sixteenth-century Spanish nobleman who came to the New World to "tame the savages" (n.p. 17) and who now blames "those Indios" (n.p. 18) for his lack of personal and professional success, including being passed over in his job at the Bureau of Indian Affairs by a Hopi administrator. After stealing a cache of gold from a traditional grave, Blud Kwan'tum is cursed, changed to a vampire who must consume the blood of full-blooded Indigenous peoples until he, too, becomes a "full-blood," thus transforming into that which he hates most. Allowing himself to be bitten, Super Indian defeats Blud Kwan'tum by poisoning him with blood tainted by Rezium.

Alluding to the "blood-quantum" laws that the governments of the United States and Canada at one time employed to determine the legal status of Indigenous peoples and their tribal rolls, Blud Kwan'tum represents yet another means of the European theft of Indigenous culture (for a useful parallel, think of Lieutenant Dunbar from the movie *Dances with Wolves*, the white savior who symbolically becomes champion for the Sioux[17]). Despite the use of such policies to determine federal recognition and inclusion on sanctioned tribal rolls, many Indigenous peoples find "blood-quantum" regulations to be another arm of settler colonialism. As Eva Marie Garroutte (2003) writes in her study *Real Indians: Identity and the Survival of Native America*, many of those "who object to legal standards of identity ignore the ways that these may affect tribal blood quanta," complaining that "legal mechanisms for establishing connections to tribal communities are culturally foreign" (35). Rather than focusing on genetic parentage and DNA, many Indigenous peoples hold that "an individual's cultural characteristics may actually take precedence over anything else in the determinations of tribal belonging" (76); in fact, as Garroutte notes, "in some cases, whole communities have collectively embraced particular individuals, even though they are not relatives by either law or blood, if they demonstrate cultural competence" (77). In short, "blood-quantum" laws are a foreign imposition on Indigenous understandings of individual and communal identity. In light of this, readers are encouraged to recognize in the character of Blud Kwan'tum a continuation of the settler-colonial impulse to bodily regulate—down to the individual level—Indigenous peoples, as well as use those communities as tools for the development of colonial desires. Blud Kwan'tum's immediate goal was to use the residents of Leaning Oak to fuel his cure, only to be defeated by another "cure" that was proffered to those same residents as a solution to hunger and malnutrition. Super Indian may thus serve metaphorically as a hero for Indigenous peoples generally, but his heroism is in service of his immediate community and its cultural values. In this way, Super Indian is very unlike Superman, who will often divert his attention away from Metropolis to take on the seemingly loftier goal of protecting people from national, international, or intergalactic enemies. For Super Indian—and for Indigenous superheroes more generally—the loftiest goal is the protection of one's immediate community.

Arigon Starr, like Theo Tso, thus uses her series to provide a new spin on the traditional figure of the superhero, focusing the acts of heroism on a smaller scale while simultaneously addressing the persistent threats to contemporary Indigenous peoples. In contrast to the Marvel and DC superheroes whose villains are, increasingly, interplanetary threats that bear little to no resemblance to the social ills faced by contemporary American society, Super Indian exists to combat the persistence of colonial efforts that work to decimate Indigenous culture and imprison—or erase—Indigenous peoples. Starr's (2012, 2015a) efforts to support actual Indigenous peoples is further marked by her inclusion of biographical sketches of "Real Super Indians" (*passim*) bringing to her readers' attention the accomplishments of significant Indigenous individuals in a variety of professions. With biographies of famed New York City Ballet prima ballerina Maria Tallchief (Osage); Jim Thorpe (Sac and Fox), often referred to as "the greatest athlete of the twentieth century"; media icon Will Rogers (Cherokee); Susan LaFlesche Picotte (Omaha), "the first female Native American doctor in the United States"; and Moses Yellowhorse (Pawnee), MLB's first full-blooded Native American pitcher, Starr is using her series to promote the efforts of what we might call "everyday heroes," historical figures whose lives can serve to inspire her readership, particularly her young Indigenous readers. For all that myth-like figures such as Super Indian make for engaging storytelling and inspire readers to greatness, it's the heroics of real people that actually improve the world. One can fantasize about becoming a superhero, but one can actually work toward becoming a leader in one's community.

• • •

While there are exciting ongoing series currently being published, there are earlier stand-alone works that are also worthy of serious attention. For instance, Jay Odjick's (Kitigan Zibi Anishinabe) graphic novel *Kagagi: The Raven*[18] uses the genre of the superhero comic to creatively retell the story of the windigo, a people-eating creature popular in traditional Anishinabe stories. Forged in battle against the windigo and its forces of destruction, "one young Anishinabe warrior [named Wisakedjak[19]] who had lost all to the beast would lead them" to victory (Odjick 2010, n.p. 4). This hero survives from the times before European conquest to the modern day, eventually passing on his mantle—and his powers—to an unsuspecting high-school student who, much like Peter Parker, is bullied by the star athlete in his class and mocked as a nerd. A chance encounter with a minion of the windigo revealed to young Matt his heroic nature, in part by means of the MPI matrix noted above: the windigo's minion calls him by the name Kagagi, and the attacks against him draw out both Matt's previously unknown powers as well as his superhero costume, a black suit with wing-like straps on the arm bands, befitting a hero whose namesake is a raven (figure 1.5). The dark suit and black armored gloves, as well as the cartoonish "Krak!" accompanying the punch, call to mind Batman, who also often operates at night, outside of the bounds of the legal system, and does so in order to protect the community he calls home. As such, Odjick is using the visual rhetoric of classic comic-book superheroes to help his audiences best understand the context for his new hero.

By the end of the book, Matt and "Jack" have defeated the forces of the windigo while noting that the danger has only been kept at bay temporarily, thus suggesting the need for the older hero to pass on

Figure 1.5. Jay Odjick, *Kagagi: The Raven*.

his mantle, common among such superheroes as the Green Lantern Corps. The book ends with the two heroes supporting each other, with the elder promising to answer all of Matt's questions about his powers and their history. Although this book is little more than an origin story, one important point the reader is left with is the fact that Kagagi's purpose in the present—like Wisakedjak's purpose in the past—is to protect his tribal community from an evil force bent on that community's destruction. Rooted in Anishinabe folklore rather than contemporary reservation politics, *Kagagi* employs the figure of the superhero as a contemporary version of the traditional figure of Wisakedjak, who is further modernized by wearing a leather jacket and riding a motorcycle. Odjick is thus suggesting that "superheroes" have long been part of traditional Indigenous narratives rather than being a new invention. Just as the windigo is "the darkness that resides in the blackest nightmares of all the Anishinabe," he is also the arch-nemesis for the "superhero" Wisakedjak who, much like the Green Lantern, can pass his powers on to a worthy successor. Possessing the

requisite array of traits to satisfy the MPI matrix—his mission is to
stop the windigo, his powers include super strength and force beams
directed from his fists, and his black costume manifests when the
windigo appears—Kagagi bears all the markers of a contemporary
superhero as well as a traditional Anishinabe hero. Although only one
volume of the book was published, Kagagi was later adapted as an
animated television show of the same name that aired in Canada on
APTN Kids (which provides Indigenous-created children's program-
ming) in 2014, thus taking on new life beyond the pages of the comic
while also providing more representation for Indigenous superheroes
across multiple media platforms.

In another, much more poignant example, originally published
in 1996, *Tribal Force* has recently been rereleased (with some minor
alterations) by the Native Realities Press. Composed by Jon Proudstar
(Yaqui), the single-issue comic focuses on the young Nita, a survivor
of child molestation who summons the superhero Thunder Eagle
through an act of meta-narrative by drawing him in her own comic
artwork. Bearing a symbol on his chest alluding to the Ghost Dance—
"a tribute to the countless murdered souls from which he draws his
immense power" (Proudstar 2017, n.p. 12)—Thunder Eagle bears a
name, a mission, and an array of powers that clearly provides the
necessary MPI matrix possessed by other comic-book superheroes.[20]
However, as the narrator tells us early on: "Just to be clear, this isn't
a story about heroes. It's a story about monsters" (n.p. 7). Following
these words, the reader is brought to Nita's home, where an unidentified male authority figure commands the young girl to first take off
her jacket and then remove her pants "nice and slow," suggesting his
intention of sexual abuse. Inspired by the hero she has been drawing,
Nita stands up to this man, demanding that he stop touching her,
or this hero will "make war on you" (n.p. 10). In response, the man
assaults Nita who, lying on the ground bleeding, whispers for Thunder
Eagle's help (figure 1.6). Note also that the man has been drinking,
suggesting that alcohol is part of the underlying problem Nita (and,
likely, her larger community) is facing.

This depressing story illustrates yet another problem that reservation populations face in addition to those highlighted by *Captain
Paiute* and *Super Indian*: the abuse of those least able to protect

Figure 1.6. Jon Proudstar, *Tribal Force*, no. 1.

themselves (particularly children).[21] And like reservation politics more broadly, this issue is also largely unaddressed by superhero comics; even those heroes, like Batman, Spider-Man, and Daredevil, who regularly turn their attention to what might be called "common criminals" (as opposed to supervillains) do not spend many pages hunting down child molesters. In an author's statement following the narrative, Proudstar (2017) notes, "For the past twenty-five years, I have worked with Survivors of Child Molestation and Violent Youth Offenders" and that his comic book comes out of his need to present this issue to his readers. More than just a graphic illustration of contemporary social ills, however, this book is also an explicit call to action: "I know this is only a comic book but I hope somewhere, someone reads this and is motivated to make a change or speak out. . . . The responsibility of exposing these horrible acts to the light of day has been left to us" (n.p. 16). With his comic series (he suggests in his author's note that there will be more issues in the future, though none have been released as of this writing), Proudstar makes explicit what Tso and Starr imply: Indigenous comics are more than just engaging entertainment; the books address real issues, faced by real people, and call for real solutions. We cannot, in other words, just be readers; we have an obligation to act. In an interview for *High Country News*, Proudstar notes: "A lot of kids misinterpret what a warrior is. It has nothing to do with war. A warrior takes care of his village, makes sure the old ones are taken care of, and that the children are safe" (Bailer 2014, n.p.). This message is reinforced by the cover to *Tribal Force* issue 1, which pictures Thunder Eagle holding a hatchet, ready to protect a scared young girl (presumably Nita) positioned at his feet, clutching a doll. And as noted in the title, Thunder Eagle is a manifestation of a "*tribal* force," a protector of communities often ignored by law enforcement agencies as well as mainstream superheroes.[22]

In another metanarrative move by an Indigenous creator, Stephen Graham Jones's short graphic novel *My Hero*[23] spends most of its pages outlining a potential superhero story. Presented as the beginning of a project between high-school friends, the hero known as "the Staranger"24 appears to be an idea borne out of mystery (a "stranger") and the oft-employed hero from outer space (a "star ranger") such as we see in Superman and the Captain Marvel of the Marvel Cinematic

Universe. Jones (2017) additionally alludes to the larger superhero universe(s) in the opening narrative: "Bitten long ago by that radioactive bug of comic books, dynamic duo Lance & Kenneth were desperate to escape the dying planet of Cooper High and crash-land on the shelves as the mysterious **Dr. Never**, creator of the throwback sensation for which they just signed their first merchandising deal! Get ready for that bane of all evil schemes, foiler of dastardly deeds, Jell-O eating champion of **three** galaxies" (1). In this short opening, Jones references three of the most well-known comic-book superheroes: Spider-Man ("radioactive bug"), Batman ("dynamic duo"), and Superman ("escape the dying planet"), while also using Golden Age (roughly 1938–1956) turns of phrase ("dastardly deeds") and alluding to the popularity of secondary market forces ("first merchandising deal"). In this short opening, then, Jones situates his comic firmly within the genre by blatantly alluding to multiple stock tropes, as if the tropes are more important than the superhero himself, about whom we get very little information in this narrative.

My Hero is clearly a draft of a superhero comic, even if the details of his character and purpose are left unclear. In this regard, *My Hero* employs what fans of Superman might call a Bizarro-version of the MPI matrix: "the Staranger" has no secret identity (though it is suggested his name might be "Doby"), his mission is unclear (he is to save "a whole new galaxy" from an unidentified threat [Jones 2017, 11]), and his costume has not yet been designed, outside of the outline of a cape and cowl common among superheroes.

As we see in figure 1.7, the last page of the metanarrative, the Staranger exists as an outline of a hero, flying above some "random grey pipes" among the "stars everywhere, man," near an unidentified "beast of a star carrier." This final page is a larger version of a smaller panel on the first page (drawn underneath the narrative text quoted above), which includes other directions for the eventual artwork, such as "thick white letters" and "supposed to still look like half a skull," as well as the suggestion of a sidekick: "is that a space armadillo?" (Jones 2017, 1). The rest of the narrative follows suit, with panels filled in only with snippets of narrative text and instructions for artwork to be included later. Jones also demonstrates a full range of possible panels, everything from full-page spreads to pages filled with multiple smaller

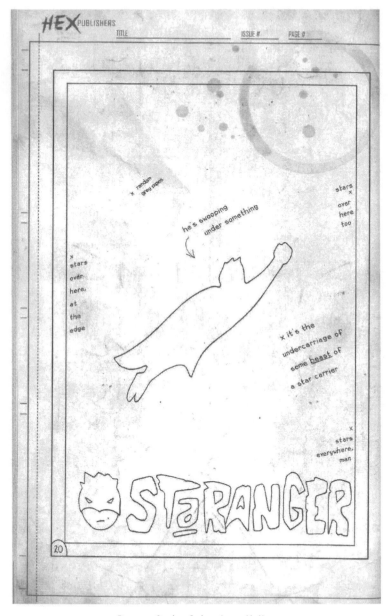

Figure 1.7. Stephen Graham Jones, *My Hero*.

panels and panels of all shapes and sizes, alluding to the diversity of compositional options employed by comics artists.[25] Further, the detail in the upper-right corner looks like the ring of a drink, with drops from said drink having spilled onto the page. The suggestion here is that the artist has been working on this page over time, perhaps drinking coffee to help stay focused on the work. This, too, is part of the process, part of the work that goes into creation.

With this incarnation of a superhero, Jones is demonstrating to his readers that, while the MPI index may be necessary for defining a superhero, readers can easily identify a superhero narrative even without the creator clearly articulating a mission, powers, or identity. Only the vaguest of outlines is enough to identify the genre and generate a compelling narrative. (Does the reader need to know why the galaxy needs saving in order to be invested? Does the reader's support of the hero wane if his powers have not yet manifested? Is anything more than the hint of a cape needed to identify the hero?) Additionally, the lack of clear characterization may allow readers to more easily see themselves in the role of the hero. Writing about Latinx comics readers, Aldama (2017) argues, "It's this capacity ["the wonderfully generative capacity of this cocreating potential in comic book readers and audiences"] that allows Latinos to imagine beyond the boundaries of Anglo superhero comics; even if Batman doesn't look like us, we can imagine ourselves as Batman" (91). By not clearly racializing the superhero (remembering that many extraterrestrial superheroes in the Marvel and DC comics are clearly racialized as white), Jones is subtly inviting his readers—all of his readers—to imagine themselves as this hero. Finally, the skeletal narrative outline and notes also serve as an invitation to the readers to compose their own superhero comics. Where the finished product—the sharply drawn images, the bright coloring, and the stylized lettering (all often generated by separate professionals working in collaboration with the writer)—might seem daunting to young would-be creators, a rough outline is certainly a more achievable goal and may inspire readers to design their own superheroes and pen their own narratives. Additionally, the short narrative that follows this metanarrative—titled "Hey, Stranger" and ostensibly penned by "Ken-Bot, the mechanical pencil" (Jones 2017, n.p. 23)—shows two teenagers at a funeral who come together at the appearance of an armadillo-themed superhero (a manifestation of the "space armadillo" referenced on the first page of *My Hero*); the final panel then shows a brightly-colored, caped superhero action figure leaning against a grave (possibly the Staranger, although he does not wear a skull-like mask, as indicated in the metanarrative outline).[26]

The Staranger and his sidekick are clearly identified as coming from outer space, and nothing in the text marks the setting as a reservation—or other tribal—community. As such, *My Hero* breaks with the above works by not focusing on Indigenous superheroes, Indigenous communities, and reservations. However, the book does repeatedly refer to collaborative acts and community building, which do underlie all the above superhero narratives: cocreation, collaborative hero work, the coming together as a community to mourn a death, and the team building suggested at the appearance of the space armadillo. But more importantly, *My Hero* demonstrates that Indigenous creators should not feel compelled to only write about Indigenous peoples and communities, and such a limitation may inadvertently curtail the kinds of freedoms that have never been applied to white comics creators. As important as Indigenous superheroes are to the genre itself as well as to Indigenous audiences, Indigenous creators also have imagination, the creative capacity, and the freedom to compose any stories of their choosing. In short, no one racial population owns the right to create a superhero from outer space.[27]

• • •

The ubiquitous appeal of superhero comics has also been employed by comics writers who are otherwise not writing within the genre. And like some of his contemporaries, Gord Hill (Kwakwaka'wakw) alludes to superhero comics for explicitly political reasons. Perhaps most well-known for his books *The 500 Years of Resistance Comic Book* and *The Anti-Capitalist Resistance Comic Book*, Hill has cultivated a reputation for being blatantly political, using graphic novels to educate his readers about pressing contemporary political problems while simultaneously documenting the relevant history. Composed of short vignettes presenting moments from first contact through the late twentieth century, from Indigenous communities throughout

North America, *The 500 Years of Resistance Comic Book* documents the history of armed resistance against European invaders and the continuation of settler-colonial domination by their descendants (Hill 2010). *The Anti-Capitalist Resistance Comic Book* similarly documents protests against capitalism, an economic system at the heart of settler-colonial domination that has negatively affected the vast majority of all North Americans (Hill 2012). And in *The Antifa Comic Book: 100 Years of Fascism and Antifa Movements*, Hill (2018) broadens his reach to present to his audience the history of antifascist resistance throughout Europe before concluding with the rise of fascism in the United States (particularly following the election of Donald Trump as president in 2016). Hill's body of work, then, can be read as a narrative of settler-colonial ideology as it first affected Indigenous communities in North America, with an ever-widening scope to document the physical, economic, and political violence that continues to oppress an increasingly large number of disenfranchised peoples.

Like the first two books, *The Antifa Comic Book* is composed of short vignettes tied together thematically and presented (roughly) chronologically, providing for the reader an easy-to-read graphic history of antifascist resistance. However, unlike the first two books, the forward (written by Mark Bray[28]) opens with an explicit reference to superhero comics. Invoking *Captain America* issue 1 (1941), the cover of which depicts Captain America punching Adolf Hitler, Bray (2018) opens his introduction with: "Comic books were made for Nazi punching. The industry that Superman built in the 1930s became intimately interwoven into American war propaganda during World War II. As Wonder Woman and Batman supported the war effort, they were joined by the wildly popular Captain America, who punched Hitler amid a hail of bullets on the first cover" (7). Although the end of his introduction complicates this narrative of comics' history of political protest by noting, "Although early superheroes opposed Nazism, they did so in the interest of preserving that status quo that gave birth to it in the first place" (12), Bray's opening invocation of the comic-book industry's literal depiction of punching Nazis serves multiple purposes. First, Bray reminds the readers that antifascist movements are nothing new (despite conservative media's desire to frame "antifa" as a contemporary reaction to the rise of Donald Trump) and that

THE FIRST SIGNIFICANT *ANTI-FASCIST* RESISTANCE OCCURRED IN SEPTEMBER 1933, WHEN SEVERAL *HUNDRED* B.U.F. MEMBERS ATTEMPTED TO MARCH IN *STOCKTON* IN NORTHEAST ENGLAND.

SOME *2,000* ANTI-FASCISTS *ATTACKED* THE RALLY AND *FORCED* THE BLACKSHIRTS TO *DISPERSE*, INJURING *20* OF THEM IN THE PROCESS. THIS AND OTHER CLASHES LED TO A *DECLINE* IN PUBLIC SUPPORT FOR THE B.U.F., WHICH BY 1935 HAD JUST *8,000* MEMBERS.

Figure 1.8. Gord Hill, *The Antifa Comic Book: 100 Years of Fascism and Antifa Movements.*

depictions of such efforts have long been a part of American popular culture. Further, American superheroes—from Superman and his unquestioned moral character to the dark vigilante Batman to the overtly patriotic Captain America—have always been shown to oppose fascism. But perhaps most importantly, this opening allusion normalizes the violence in a way that may suggest to his readers that they too should punch Nazis.[29]

This suggestion is emphasized by Hill's artwork throughout the book. The front cover—perhaps also alluding to *Captain America* issue 1, given that the fascist is drawn to resemble Hitler—depicts a masked antifa protester punching a fascist distributing alt-right pamphlets. Throughout the book, Hill depicts a variety of antifa protests, with many examples of individual protesters punching members of fascist groups, including the now-infamous example of an unidentified protester punching white nationalist Richard Spencer while the latter was giving a live, on-camera interview with the Australian Broadcasting Corporation about Donald Trump's inauguration. Hill similarly connects these acts of protest to superhero comics by depicting them with the ubiquitous brightly colored, spiked shape employed by comics artists to register that a punch has been delivered (figure 1.8). This small detail is a subtle nod to the kind of comics imagery (also alluded to in figure 1.5, above) that presents necessary, even justified violence that superheroes commit in order to protect their communities. Hill is subtly suggesting here that punching Nazis is just such an act of violence.

Readers familiar with the history of superhero comics to which Bray alludes in the introduction will no doubt recognize this visual signification and further read the antifa protesters as engaged in the same kind of hero work as Captain America. This connection becomes strengthened by Hill's (2018) similar use of words like "KABOOM" to depict explosions (85). And it should be noted that, while there are many reasons that *The Antifa Comic Book* could be Hill's first graphic novel to employ a color palette instead of black and white, the use of a color scheme reminiscent of the Golden Age of comics only solidifies for the audience the connection between superheroes and antifascist work.

• • •

As Mark Bray and Gord Hill remind us, superhero comics have long been vehicles for political commentary. That said, creators like Theo Tso, Arigon Starr, and Jon Proudstar highlight the relatively small scope of political concerns addressed by mainstream superhero comics, consistently ignoring Indigenous peoples and their struggles against settler colonialism; similarly, Jay Odjick brings to light the connections between traditional tribal stories and superhero comics, alluding to a rich narrative mine that yet remains untapped. Even explicitly apolitical (and possibly antinarrative) work like Stephen Graham Jones's can—when included as part of the larger Indigenous revisioning of the genre of superhero comics—be read for its work in encouraging community efforts in the arts (an issue we will return to in chapter 4). Whether composing comics that develop a new Indigenous superhero figure or alluding to the larger history of superhero comics to make an important (aesthetic or political) point—such as challenging "the genre's eighty-plus-year history" of superhero comics that Jeffrey A. Brown (2020) notes has been "overwhelmingly white"

(389)—Indigenous superhero comics focus on the importance of community, whether explicitly or implicitly doing so as a response to the machinery of settler colonialism that has pushed Indigenous peoples to the margins of society and ignored their concerns in many forms of popular media. In this regard, Indigenous creators are not merely creating Indigenous heroes but are actively confronting the industry's history of avoiding race and ethnicity; as Brown also notes, "More often than not, superheroes have avoided ethnicity as a topic" (390). For Indigenous creators, race is central to the identity of the superhero. As socially conscious as they are entertaining, as much activist stances as artistic creations, Indigenous superhero comics reimagine the traditional figure of the mainstream comic-book superhero and call for political action in the face of the real dangers faced by Indigenous peoples in North America. We will see the same issues mirrored in the following chapter, which focuses on science fiction narratives. As with superhero narratives, science fiction narratives have long enjoyed popular appeal and have been a vehicle for successful political commentary. And as with the comics creators discussed in this chapter, Indigenous creators of science fiction comics have recently employed them as a vehicle for profound antisettler-colonial commentary.

CHAPTER 2

INDIGENOUS TRAVELS IN SPACE, TIME, AND TECHNOLOGY

If you start a conversation about science fiction with somebody, chances are they will have much to say. And while it's true that not everybody is a fan of such series as *Star Wars* and *Star Trek*,[1] you'd be hard-pressed to find somebody who isn't familiar with those immensely popular, globally distributed franchises. In my experience, even those people who have never seen a single film or television episode can still talk with some familiarity about the Skywalker family and the crew of the Enterprise, given their ubiquity in popular culture (especially in English-speaking North America). I have yet to meet a person who cannot name at least the major characters and who does not recognize either the *Millennium Falcon* or the *Enterprise*, even if they cannot name those ships. But even those few who are wholly unfamiliar with these franchises can still picture science fiction television and films, with plucky crews of explorers traveling through outer space to discover new planets and engage in thrilling battles armed with laser-beam technology. However, despite the relative ease with which many if not most people can bring to mind such images, relatively few of them will populate those images with Indigenous peoples. When one considers the almost complete lack of Indigenous representation in most science fiction franchises—with the notable exception that "encountering indigenous aliens who become hostile" remains a popular trope in science fiction—it's certainly not surprising that many people do not include Native American or First Nations peoples in their mental conceptions of interstellar adventuring.[2] Further, as Roger Luckhurst (2005) reminds us in his cultural history of the genre, "science fiction is a literature of technologically saturated societies" (3);

although the material realities of many reservations may suggest a lack of technological saturation, we must remember that Indigenous peoples live in—and consume the media developed in—the colonizing nations they are situated within. Similarly, given the general mindset that Indigenous peoples are most often associated with the past rather than the future—more easily imagined in westerns than in any other popular genre—we can understand why Indigenous peoples are rarely associated with a technologically advanced future.[3]

It is for these reasons that more attention must be paid to Indigenous-authored science fiction. And as Miriam C. Brown Spiers (2021) claims, "Indigenous science fiction—science fiction written by Indigenous authors, as opposed to science fiction that simply includes Indigenous characters—is a relatively new genre" (xi). As such, now is the time to begin exploring the myriad dimensions of the narratives being produced, some of which work in wildly different ways from the narratives discussed below. While it is true that "science fiction" as a genre encompasses so much more than narratives of space travel often set in the future,[4] I choose to narrow my focus to this one aspect of science fiction for two reasons. First, there is a sizeable—and growing—number of such works being published, and I wish to treat those works as participating in a larger movement. Scientifically advanced space travel is a staple of speculative fiction that shares much with such subgenres as steampunk and artificial-intelligence fiction.[5] However, I would argue that narratives of space travel are what most people think of when thinking about science fiction. Second, and more importantly, these works provide an important political commentary on the role of Indigenous people in narratives about the future. The works discussed below all participate in a larger conversation about the viability of Indigenous survivance, what Gerald Vizenor (2009) characterizes as "an active sense of presence over absence, deracination, and oblivion," in stories that are "renunciations of dominance, detractions, obtrusions, the unbearable sentiments of tragedy, and the legacy of victimry" (85). As a whole, works of Indigenous science fiction that are projected into the future and/or engage with technological innovations not yet realized could be said to comprise a subset of survivance narratives; such narratives envision a future that take for granted the continuation of Indigenous peoples and their stories and, as such, embody Vizenor's (2009) assertion that "Native survivance is a continuance of stories" (1), as well as demonstrating Spiers's (2021) claim that Indigenous science fiction "has the ability to challenge and expand the mainstream critical definitions of the genre itself" (xii). Further, some of the following narratives suggest the potential of a future that includes "Indigenous nationhood," which Leanne Betasamosake Simpson (2017; Mississauga Nishnaabeg) asserts "is a radical and complete overturning of the nation-state's political formations" (10); in other words, although perhaps not explicitly so, some of the stories below suggest a future where Indigenous peoples are no longer subject to the machinations of settler colonialism. These works all provide a story as well as a visual representation of Indigenous peoples in a future that holds more opportunities for self-determination and advancement than does the present situation for many still addressing the various limitations imposed by settler colonialism. As we will see, Indigenous peoples are leaders of expeditionary missions as well as scientifically advanced masters of technologies not yet invented. In addition to the "representation" that often ends when stereotypes are finally given a lead role (after, say, four previous installments of a popular American television franchise that included African American and Asian American representation from the start), these works also provide an underlying narrative of political protest and social advancement that matches the sense of hope for the future that much science fiction—especially those works devoted to the exploration of outer space—encourage in their readers.

Despite the fact that, like comics more generally, "science fiction is typically regarded as a low literary form, often completely ignored or edged to the margin of literary study of intellectual history as rather juvenile" (Luckhurst 2005, 2), scholars like Isiah Lavender III and DeWitt Douglas Kilgore have focused their attention on not just the aesthetics of the genre but on its use as a vehicle for political commentary, particularly with respect to race. In his *Race in American Science Fiction*, Lavender (2011) claims that "science fiction is actually transmitting assumptions of racism even in stories that are ostensibly envisioning a future where race has become irrelevant" (20); that is to say, while much science fiction may project a promise of what we might now call a "postracial" world, the lack of direct engagement with racial tensions merely hides underlying racist assumptions. For Lavender, science fiction "seems to be uniquely suited to the critical study of race" given its explicit employment of different species—as well as "exotic landscapes"—but fails to do so by paying "scant attention to the relationship" (10) between these various peoples and their homelands. That is to say, much American (and Canadian) science fiction uncritically employs the social and political assumptions of race without challenging those underlying assumptions, despite being perfectly situated to do so. Lavender (2014b) clarifies this point later, in the introduction to his collection *Black and Brown Planets: The Politics of Race in Science Fiction*[6] when he notes that "the link between race and politics in science fiction is always evident but is most often confined to explorations of how racial identity inflects or challenges conventional narrative expectations" (6); that is to say, race will appear as a theme in the narrative, as a means of highlighting or subverting narrative expectations, but is not itself the focus of or explored in depth by the narrative.[7]

Similarly, in his *Astrofuturism: Science, Race, and Visions of Utopia in Space*, Kilgore (2003) defines astrofuturism as "the tradition of speculative fiction and science writing inaugurated by scientists and science popularizers during the space race of the 1950s." And as much as this reflects a period of significant technological advancement—especially in the United States—we must also remember that the "space race" was very much a "raced space" (2). Kilgore explicitly notes that "this study is positioned against the conceit that science and technology have little to do with political, economic, and social issues" (5). While there certainly may have been a time when writers and readers alike may have convinced themselves of the apolitical nature of science fiction—if not speculative fiction more generally—we have long since abandoned that notion.[8] However, often, those seemingly apolitical works were still "based on a series of exclusions," exclusions which were certainly "raced and gendered" (10); that is, even without addressing politics directly (or even metaphorically), a great deal of science fiction focused exclusively on the adventures of white men from economically secure and technologically advanced societies. For Kilgore, "racial difference" is central to astrofuturism; however, his articulation of that centrality is equally—if subtly—problematic:

"If the wonderful dream of the space frontier is the American Dream writ large, then it is appropriate to ask the same questions of it that we have asked of its terrestrial counterpart" (10). The "American dream," of course, is not a "wonderful dream" for those who were consciously excluded from the march of Manifest Destiny.[9] Indigenous peoples of North America, of course, were the victims of Manifest Destiny and remain the victims of the ongoing machinery of settler colonialism that—in large part—was built out of the promise of the "American dream" for white Americans.

That science fiction has long operated as a vehicle for narratives of colonialism should come as no surprise given the broad outlines of both space-based science fiction and the project of Manifest Destiny: an invading alien force "discovers" a new land, claims it as its own, and then proceeds to settle that land while displacing the original inhabitants. John Rieder (2008) makes such a connection when he argues that science fiction "estranges the colonial gaze by reversing the direction of the gaze's anachronism—science fiction pictures a possible future instead of the past" (10).[10] Further, this colonial gaze is built on the "ideological fantasies" that emerge from science fiction, including the "discoverer's fantasy," the "missionary fantasy" (31), and the "anthropologist's fantasy" (32), all of which situate the Indigenous inhabitants as Other. As such, much canonical science fiction situates Indigeneity as doubly removed—historically past and culturally Other—thus allowing for their erasure. However, his exploration of the colonial roots of canonical science fiction does not include an analysis of any such works produced by the colonized. As we will see below, Indigenous authors of science fiction[11] employ and repurpose many of the tropes of science fiction—including the colonial gaze itself—to confront and reject their erasure under settler colonialism, whether Indigenous peoples are themselves the explorers of outer space or space fantasies are explicitly used to preserve cultural heritage.

Although there is a distinct lack of scholarly focus on Indigenous science fiction (Spiers's [2021] book, noted above, is a welcome intervention on the subject), two related lines of inquiry can provide a roadmap for better understanding the complex narrative and socio-political aspects of such work: those focused on Afrofuturism and Indigenous futurisms.[12] Reynaldo Anderson (2015) provides an excellent history of Afrofuturism in his article "Critical Afrofuturism: A Case Study in Visual Rhetoric, Sequential Art, and Postapocalyptic Black Identity," which brings that critical history to bear on the study of Afrofuturist comics. For Anderson, "Critical Afrofuturist theory operates from a standpoint that intersects theories of time and space, technology, class, race, gender, and sexuality and delineates a general economy of racialization in relation to forces of production and apocalyptic, dystopian, and utopian futures" (183). Recognizing the importance of technology as a component of identity, Afrofuturism not only considers how Black people are imagined as participants in a technologically advanced future but also focuses on the means by which these imagined futures racialize Black people, given its ability to "interrogate the fallacies, hypocrisies, and conceits of the so-called postracial moment" (190). André M. Carrington (2016) continues this line of thinking when he notes in his study *Speculative Blackness: The Future of Race in Science Fiction* that "formerly enslaved peoples have crafted alternatives to realism and positivism as approaches to history" in the "construction of future pasts" (183). That is to say, while recognizing the history of enslavement that is central to Black diasporic peoples, Afrofuturism is not bound to repeat that history or even limit itself to seemingly logical developments from that past.

Indigenous futurisms, as articulated by Grace L. Dillon (Anishi-naabe), operate similarly. In the introduction to her collection of global Indigenous science fiction, *Walking the Clouds*, Dillon (2012) writes of "Native slipstream," which she defines as "a species of specu-lative fiction within the science fiction realm [that] infuses stories with time travel, alternative realities and multiverses, and alternative histories" (3). Informed simultaneously by traditional epistemologies as well as projections of technological developments, Dillon makes it clear that "Native slipstream thinking . . . has been around for millen-nia, anticipat[ing] recent cutting-edge physics, ironically suggesting that Natives have had things right all along" (4).[13] And whereas Dil-lon apparently suggests a continuum between the past, present, and future, science fiction novelist Rebecca Roanhorse (Pueblo[14]) more clearly connects these concepts while erasing their differences. In her essay "Postcards from the Apocalypse," Roanhorse (2018) writes that the past "is folded into the present, which is folded into the future—a philosophical wormhole that renders the very definitions of time and space fluid in the imagination."[15] Rather than moving on from the past, "Indigenous Futurism rewrites the past to reimagine the present" (n.p.) and, in doing so, is clearly commenting on the present lives of contemporary Indigenous peoples.

For Roanhorse (2018), this present moment is "a zombie apocalypse," a metaphor drawn from speculative fiction to explain living under the continued operations of settler colonialism, which promotes the "tendency to talk about the Indigenous inhabitants of North America in the past tense," a tendency that "reinforces the narrative that we are all dead" (n.p.).[16] As we will see below, the graphic novelists producing science fiction narratives all confront—to varying degrees—the machinery of settler colonialism while rejecting the narrative that would suggest that Indigenous peoples are not part of our technologically advanced future.[17] That said, Dillon (2012) reminds us, "Native writers who choose to experiment with science fiction . . . confront the possibility of internal colonization, a semiotic of resistance and oppression that does little to address larger historical realities that have inalterably changed Native existence" (5–6). That is to say, Indigenous writers are not only grappling with the material reality of existence under settler colonialism but are also writing in a genre that has historically worked to promote settler colonialism; many narratives of space travel, for example, are not even metaphors of colonization but rather loosely fictionalized reenactments of European first contact with Indigenous peoples and places.[18] For this reason Dillon, employing language that would be later echoed by Roanhorse, also argues that "all forms of Indigenous futurisms are narratives of *biskaabiiyang*, an Anishinaabemowin word connoting the process of 'returning to ourselves,' which involves discovering how personally one is affected by colonization, discarding the emotional and psychological baggage carried from its impact, and recovering ancestral traditions in order to adapt in our post-Native Apocalypse world" (10). In short, Indigenous futurisms are not merely an imagining of Indigenous peoples in a technologically advanced future but a complex negotiation of traditional knowledges and future possibilities, a reclamation of identity stripped away by colonization and reformed in its continued presence, simultaneously personal and communal.

This chapter will open with an analysis of multiple short pieces collected in the various *Moonshot* collections: Cree writer Todd Houseman's "Ayanisach," Ojibway writer Jennifer Storm and Cree writer/illustrator Kyle Charles's "Future World," Caddo writer and scholar Michael Sheyahshe and Cherokee writer/illustrator Roy Boney Jr.'s "Xenesi: The Traveler," Port Gamble S'Klallam artist Jeffrey Veregge's "Journeys," and Kickapoo multimedia artist Arigon Starr and Qalipu Mi'kmaq illustrator David Cutler's "Ue-Pucase: Water Master." These will be followed by an analysis of Richard Crowsong,[19] Derrick B. Lee (Chíshí/Diné), and Tristen Oakenthorn's (Lakota/Nimiipuu) book *S9: Sequoyah 9* and Tahltan artist Cole Pauls's limited series *Dakwäkãda Warriors*.

• • •

The communal approach to the use of comics as a means of addressing settler colonialism is perhaps best illustrated by the *Moonshot* collections. Funded by a Kickstarter project in 2015, the original *Moonshot* collection was quite ambitious: to collect short, new comics from some of the best Indigenous comics creators from throughout North America. With established writers and artists who have worked on mass-market titles, as well as rising stars with as-yet-little national attention, *Moonshot* received nearly $75,000 (CAD) from over 1,500 hundred backers (Alternate History Comics Inc., n.d.-a). By the time of the third volume, released in 2019, the Kickstarter project received nearly $84,000 (CAD) from nearly 1,400 backers (Alternate History Comics Inc., n.d.-b). If the necessity for crowd-sourced funding demonstrates the difficulty Indigenous creators face in a publishing market hungry for comics and graphic novels, the number of backers and amounts raised (in both cases, exceeding their posted goals) are ample evidence of an enthusiastic audience. Collecting work representing a wide variety of artistic styles—from cartoonish to photorealistic to abstract—these volumes can also serve as an introduction to comic-book art more generally, thus demonstrating the phenomenal range of Indigenous artists working today.[20] Additionally, the popularity of science fiction narratives among Indigenous creators—visions of the future here on Earth as well as exciting adventures into outer space—is reflected both in their presence in all three volumes as well as the third volume's specific focus on Indigenous futurisms.

One key component to Indigenous futurisms—as well as a central motif to much science fiction more generally—is an imagining of the future, whether a near future in which technological developments we are currently working on are realized or the far future of speculative imagination. However, unlike much of what we might call traditional science fiction's attempts to leave the past behind (except, perhaps, as metaphor), Indigenous science fiction set in the future actively incorporates the past given the centrality of the past and the refusal of linear chronology suggested by Roanhorse's comments above. One such science fiction narrative that consciously ties together the past and future is Todd Houseman's (2015; Cree) "Ayanisach," illustrated by Ben Shannon. *Ayanisach* is Cree for "he who tells stories of the past," and the story accordingly "recounts the invasion of Earth by an alien race known as 'Disrespectors'" (133), who brought destruction to the planets and its inhabitants in their relentless search for natural resources to exploit. Very clearly retelling the story of European first contact with Indigenous North America, "Ayanisach" does not merely repeat that narrative with a futuristic setting. Such a story would suggest to the reader that the future—particularly for Indigenous peoples—holds nothing but more colonial domination. Rather, we learn about Maskwa, a "great chief" who "created a war lodge" (135) to lead her people against the invaders. Driven off (presumably because of the resistance as well as the need to find other resource-heavy worlds), the Disrespectors left behind significant environmental damage as well as a diminished population. However, all the survivors depicted in the narrative appear to be Indigenous, and the final image suggests that only Indigenous peoples survived. The narrative recounts this history in front of a fire, around which many Indigenous peoples—some dressed in various "traditional" pieces, such as beaded jackets and headdresses—sit. The final panel (figure 2.1) gives a wider shot, showing this gathering to be taking place in London, in sight of Big Ben and a demolished double-decker bus.

The absence of white people in a major European capital—one which metonymically stands in for the entire British Empire and its history of global colonization—suggests that the ones who

Figure 2.1. Todd Houseman, "Ayanisach," *Moonshot*, vol. 1.

survived the Disrespectors are Indigenous, presumably those who are—who have long been—equipped to survive and thrive under various, ongoing colonizing efforts. And the means of survival are very clearly stated: "Knowing our past will ultimately take us to the future" (Houseman 2015, 138). In one respect, stories like "Ayanisach" are revolutionary for simply depicting Indigenous peoples in the future and, here, for imagining a future that may *only* be populated by Indigenous peoples. However, and perhaps more importantly, such stories embody the spirit of survivance and suggest a way to a life beyond settler colonialism. As such, works of Indigenous science fiction—especially those in comic-book art that visually represent these futures in aesthetic styles that, as we will see below, can be read as new ways of quite literally seeing our future—become powerful political statements meant to inspire as much as entertain, confronting the lived realities of settler colonization with reminders of achrono-logical representations of Indigenous peoples: the characters' dress in "Ayanisach" is meant to visually situate the past as contiguous with the future, and this is done on the same page that an elder explicitly reminds the reader of the importance of the past. This is a recurring theme we will see throughout the works discussed below.

Devoted explicitly to narratives of Indigenous futurism, the third volume of *Moonshot* also includes futuristic narratives that explicitly dismiss the linearity of time through different kinds of time travel. In "Future World," Jennifer Storm (Ojibway) and Kyle Charles (2019; Cree) imagine the year 2171 as a time filled with advanced technology but devoid of a healthy ecosystem. The narrator notes, "People are no longer allowed outside in this inhospitable environment" (11), so all interactions with the natural world must take place virtually. Our unnamed focal character loads up a simulation that allows her to converse with "the Elder," a program that situates the narrator in a virtual forest to listen to traditional tribal stories. However, "a malfunction" (15) allows the simulated Elder and the focal character to interact fully rather than a virtual reality experience where the Elder program speaks but cannot otherwise engage. Recognizing the malfunction as "breaking down a barrier in time" (16), the focal character takes this opportunity to warn the Elder of the environmental destruction to come. Like the reader, the focal character knows this is not a "malfunction, but rather a retelling of the traditional story of Spider Woman." The "malfunction" occurs when a woman came down from the sky "like she was a spider" (14); this woman, of course, is our focal character, who has been fully inserted into the simulation as opposed to situated as a witness to the digitally constructed events. Likely based on the weblike image in the background, as the figure descends from above, the Elder immediately identifies the woman from the future as Spider Woman and vows to share her warnings about the future widely, "with the future generations [of] Turtle Island" (figure 2.2).

Time travel, here, is used to call into question temporal linearity by having an individual from the mythic past come to be recast as a person from the future, who takes advantage of a "malfunction" to educate the Elder. Just as the notion of temporal linearity is turned on its head, so too is the relationship of the two central characters: where the focal character seeks to learn from the Elder, by the end of the story, the woman—now revealed to be Spider Woman—is educating the Elder. And while one level of this story can be read as a creative retelling of the story of Spider Woman, who serves as a protector of the people and is often remembered by weaving protective charms (in what have now come to be popularized—and often cheapened, by non-Indigenous creators—as dreamcatchers), readers are also invited to understand this story as a reminder that, when we ignore the past, we do so at our peril. The rush to technological advancement—a staple trope in science fiction narratives as well as one of the defining national imperatives of settler-colonial nations, such as the United States—comes at the expense of the natural world; and so long as the natural world is associated with the past—itself a common trope among representations of Indigenous peoples—our future is doomed.

Similarly, Michael Sheyahshe's (2019; Caddo) "Xenesi: The Traveler," illustrated by Cherokee artist Roy Boney Jr., tells the story of a literal time traveler, an explorer from a technologically developed future who travels back in time in order to "correct all the things space-time gets wrong" (99). Explicitly engaged in correcting past mistakes in the way that "Future World" alludes to, we begin to see a trend in Indigenous science fiction comics: the need for Indigenous peoples to "fix" a world ravaged by the machinery—in this case, the literal, technological machinery—of settler colonialism. Wearing futuristic

Figure 2.2. Jennifer Storm and Kyle Charles, "Future World," *Moonshot*, vol. 3.

armbands decorated with tribal imagery (an aesthetic associated with Indigenous futurism, which we will see more explicitly employed below) and adorned with futuristic ear plugs that suggest a technological update of traditional jewelry, Xenesi travels through time and space in a ship that appears to be a hybrid pecan tree/machine that visually suggests the harmonious coexistence of advanced technology and the natural world (figure 2.3).

Unlike Spider Woman, Xenesi does not instruct those he visits about the future; at one point, he explicitly notes, "I know you won't understand any of this now . . . but you will someday" (101) while helping an injured Caddo in 826 AD. He then continues his efforts at correction in other times: 987 AD, 1859 AD, and finally, at a point "thousands of years ago" (106), while also briefly traveling to a place called Earth-6, and a time 564 years "PT"—"Post-Terraform"

Figure 2.3. Michael Sheyahshe, "Xenesi: The Traveler," *Moonshot*, vol. 3.

(103)—suggesting a future that continues the settler-colonial impulse through the science fiction premise of terraforming, or changing other planets to suit the needs of humans.

While the temporal manipulations are more explicit in "Xenesi: The Traveler" than in "Future World," the allusion to the mythic past is far more subtle while serving the same ends. At the end of the story, a curious young Caddo boy sneaks aboard Xenesi's ship. Rather than become angry, Xenesi instead welcomes the boy on board and promises to teach him how to use the technology. In the story's final panel, we learn that the boy is named Táshah, Caddo for "coyote." While it's very likely that this boy is simply named after the popular trickster figure and is not that figure himself, the boy's origins "deep in the earth, thousands of years ago" (106)—in both a time and a place not definitively specified but situated long before recorded history—could, in fact, make him the famous trickster. In an inventive retelling not unlike that for Spider Woman in "Future Worlds," Táshah is about to embark on a series of exciting adventures that will surely give him a great deal of knowledge and experience. Xenesi himself makes this connection explicit when he tells the boy: "you're going to have a lot of stories to tell after this. I hope your family doesn't think you're trying to TRICK them!" (107). Whether this is a retelling of the Coyote origin story or simply a boy named for the famous trickster whose adventures (and storytelling) will come to mimic that of Coyote isn't really the point. Either way, Sheyahshe uses Táshah to explicitly connect the deep past with the faraway future through an allusion to the trickster figure.[21]

In both cases, Storm and Sheyahshe compose narratives that bring figures from the future into the past, challenging the notion of time as unbreakably linear. However, in his work "Journeys," artist Jeffrey Veregge (2017; Port Gamble S'Klallam) composes a narrative that seamlessly combines them. Working largely without traditional panels to provide a narrative that isn't bound to fixed notions of space in the same way that it isn't bound to fixed notions of time, Veregge incorporates visuals that Anishinaabe artist and scholar Elizabeth LaPensée elsewhere jokingly hints at when she defines Indigenous futurisms as "alternate histories, dreaming about liquid technology, imagining a future where unceded territories are taken back, and,

Figure 2.4. Jeffrey Veregge, "Journeys," *Moonshot*, vol. 2.

ya know, space canoes" (Roanhorse et al. 2017, n.p.). While certainly
played for the joke in this line, Veregge incorporates a futuristic canoe
(figure 2.4) into his short narrative "Journeys" about space exploration
in *Moonshot*, volume 2.

Employing a geometric visual style characterized by bright colors
and strong lines, Veregge here and elsewhere[22] composes a narrative that visually captures both his tribal heritage as well as what
we might call a "traditional" science fiction aesthetic, often seen in
shows like *Star Trek*.[23] However, as we see above, he also includes
"historical" imagery with the canoe, which includes people wearing
hats reminiscent of the English colonists who settled what is now New
England (commonly called "pilgrims" in the history books), sitting
comfortably with an astronaut, all of whom are engaged in the same
work of paddling the canoe. By having the canoe transform into a
NASA space shuttle, Veregge here connects the past to the present,
while simultaneously hinting at the future, thus erasing the linear
distinctions between seemingly discrete periods of time.

The subtitle also suggests this temporal simultaneity; subtitled
"Janus" for the Roman god of (among other things) transitions and

endings, the title alludes to a god associated with movement—particularly movement through and beyond barriers—who is commonly represented with two faces, symbolically facing the past and future simultaneously. And while this reference—as well as the visual allusion to the "pilgrims"—may lead some to read this as a celebration of settler-colonial cultural history, it would be more accurate to read it as Veregge's adoption of such a history for the purposes of a survivance narrative in terms of Indigenous futurism. Rather than rejecting the cultural history of Euro-America, Veregge incorporates it into his work in order to provide a narrative of exploration that is not rooted in a desire for cultural dominance and Indigenous oppression: a narrative of what could have been as well as what could someday be in the future.[24] For starters, the explorers—who should be read as Indigenous peoples, based on the various visual and narrative cues as well as its inclusion in *Moonshot*[25]—refer to one another in terms of family relations: "uncle" and "nephew" are used instead of names, ranks, or titles. (Whether this refers to actual blood relations or a larger understanding of community as family is beside the point.) Additionally, rather than thinking of their efforts in terms of colonization (of both people and places), the explorers engage in lighthearted, teasing banter, while also noting the "connection I feel with the environment around me" (Veregge 2017, 140). Finally, the song they sing is also graphically represented, with lines of S'Klallam written out on multiple pages, including the line above the heads of the explorers in figure 2.4, visually suggesting that they are singing while paddling.[26] As such, we are encouraged to read "Janus" as a celebration of S'Klallam culture as well as a reinvention of the narrative of space exploration. In short, Veregge is suggesting that it's possible to explore without colonizing, to travel and learn in the spirit of peace and community rather than domination and exploitation.

As Veregge aptly demonstrates, interstellar travel has long been central to science fiction narratives set in the future. Long considered central to many science fiction narratives—either with humans traveling among the stars or aliens visiting Earth—physical travel between planets and galaxies is as important to Indigenous futurisms as it is to non-Indigenous science fiction. As we have seen above, many such narratives suggest that one key reason for future technological developments is to engage in such travel, immortalized in *Star Trek*'s classic phrase "to boldly go where no man has gone before."[27] However, Indigenous narratives of space travel explicitly counter the ideology of settler colonialism, an ideology that is as fundamental to science fiction as is technological development.

In "Ue-Pucase: Water Master," writer Arigon Starr (2015b; Kickapoo) and illustrator David Cutler (Qalipu Mi'kmaq) reimagine the Muscogee Creek story of "The Young Man Who Turned into a Snake" (66) as a futuristic science fiction story of space travel. Here, a traditional story used to warn people not to eat snake eggs becomes a version of *Star Trek*'s "Prime Directive," which insists on a strict noninterference policy when encountering new peoples. However, Starr takes this directive one step further: rather than prohibiting the crew from interfering with what we might call sentient beings—the (often) humanoid aliens the Enterprise regularly encounters—the "Prime Directive" in "Ue-Pucase: Water Master" prohibits the crew from interfering with the larger ecosystem.[28] Akin to the above stories, where tribal figures such as Spider Woman and Coyote are given new origin stories, Starr's short narrative retells what has become a classic premise in science fiction's most popular franchise[29] and injects it with a central component of Indigenous ideology: protection of the planet(s).

"Ue-Pucase: Water Master" opens with a spaceship traveling on an interstellar mission, whose two-man crew are clearly identified as Indigenous: in addition to being characters in a reimagined tale from traditional tribal storytelling, they are drawn with brown skin and long, black hair (one of whom wears his in a braid) to clearly identify them to the readers (figure 2.5).[30] Of course, such representation is important in science fiction narratives. As noted earlier in the chapter, Indigenous peoples are rarely represented in such narratives, and when they are, they are often little more than stereotypes. However, Starr gives her reader interstellar explorers. Even if they are "junkers" who travel from planet to planet scavenging (in what is certainly a nod to the current economic status of many Indigenous peoples), they are also clearly technologically advanced individuals who have the training and intelligence to pilot and support advanced technology for interstellar travel. That is, as much as they are metaphorically to be

Figure 2.5. Arigon Starr, "Ue-Pucase: Water Master," *Moonshot*, vol. 1.

read as "traditional" (given the story's source material), they are also representatives of an advanced human future. In short, Starr shows us Indigenous people not as relics of the past, but as hopeful images of what our society can strive to become.

We learn that the crew's version of the "Prime Directive," which the pilot calls "Junkin' 101," is "no off-world food" (Starr 2015b, 68). However, like the boy who ate the snake's eggs, the other crewman eats food he finds on this unknown planet: an old, beat-up can of SPAM, again using her futuristic science fiction narrative to subtly comment on the current situation of many Indigenous people (whose diets consist of cheap canned foods given how many reservations have become food deserts with high rates of poverty). And just as in the source material, the man who eats the SPAM quickly turns into a snake. The pilot brings his and the crewman's grandmother—dressed in a robe with a futuristic-looking collar (to accommodate a helmet dock)—who first comforts the now snake and then joins him permanently on the new world. And although nothing in the story suggests that either is in danger on this new world, the message is clear: once you engage the ecosystem of a new planet, you become part of that system. And while this is not necessarily presented as a curse—not all change is bad, of course—it does permanently change him and prohibits him from leaving the planet and continuing his adventures with the pilot.

Perhaps the most interesting—even if most subtle—part of the story, however, comes in the final panel, where the narrator (who we learn is the pilot), notes: "I'm telling you now—those old stories are true. The Creek home world is real" (Starr 2015b, 72). If the can of SPAM was not enough of a hint, this line very clearly suggests that the world these interstellar explorers found is Earth. As such, what we have here is not a story about people from Earth traveling to other planets, but rather a homecoming; people from Earth have developed the technology to leave the planet, settle on another, and spend enough time away that Earth (as we now know it) becomes little more than a distant memory, kept alive by traditional storytellers (such as the crew members' grandmother). And it's important that these interstellar travelers—these representatives from our technological future—are Indigenous. That is to say, Indigenous people not only survive into humanity's deep future but are also technologically advanced participants (if not leaders) of that future, who can bring our species back home.

In a similar vein, *S9* issue 1 provides another view of a technologically advanced Indigenous crew exploring outer space. Produced by writer and multimedia artist Richard Crowsong and illustrated by Derrick B. Lee (Chíshí/Diné) and Tristen Oakenthorn (Lakota/Nimiipuu), *S9* issue 1 is the start to what could become an exciting space adventure series. However, as noted in this book's introduction, many Indigenous artists have had trouble financing, producing, and distributing their work. As we saw above with the *Moonshot* books, Crowsong turned to the crowdfunding webpage Kickstarter to help fund his first issue (as well as the similar crowdfunding platform Indiegogo to help finance his comic *Vile*; see, respectively, Crowsong 2019; Davis, n.d.). As of this writing, the Kickstarter page is still active and promises backers a preview of issue 2, which has not yet been released. However, I am sure I am not alone in hoping this series can continue, given its exciting intervention into the science fiction genre.

Although the first issue does not give much backstory, Crowsong did provide it online, both on the Kickstarter page and, in more depth, at the former Crowsong Productions (n.d.) webpage,[31] which began as follows:

The planet's nations celebrate the 20th anniversary of the "Rapture." The event that saw the exodus of most of the planet's inhabitants to outposts such as the moon, Mars and Europa. With the Earth's resources effectively expended, the world's "First World" nations and their support nations left for "curated" outposts where their environments were altered to be inhabitable.

With the "First-world" nations abandoning Earth, many of the first nations people's [*sic*] reclaimed their former countries. Small wars broke out between communities and tribes until the Federation of 1000 Nations was formed to create work for their youth, rejuvenate the planet and live peacefully with their neighbors.

Almost immediately after the ratification of the "Turtle-Island Accord" was signed by all nations, the Earth started to recover. While still a hostile place to live because of extreme weather, the Earth was healing.

Here, we again see a major theme engaged by much Indigenous science fiction: a technologically advanced future involves environmental devastation, which is countered/corrected by Indigenous peoples. And while first left behind—suggested by the use of "Rapture" for the mass exodus—alluding to the Christian notion of God saving His chosen people, leaving behind the unworthy—Indigenous peoples also come to eventually engage in interstellar travel. However, we also learn in the online backstory that this technology was developed by Indigenous peoples "with the help of a tribal grant" and then "sold to the governments of the world" (n.p.). The backstory includes character backgrounds and descriptions of the technology (some of which differ from what is provided on the Kickstarter page), all of which suggests a much larger narrative that is still in development.

In this first issue, space diver Daniel "Buc" Proudbuck ignores the safety warnings of his captain, Doty, putting the ship and crew in danger due to unexplained and dangerous high energy readings (figure 2.6). This danger is highlighted by the lack of traditional panels, instead showing Buc floating in unrestricted space. (Doty, by contrast, is safely aboard the ship and represented in the one traditional panel on the page.) Additionally, in the middle of this crisis, Doty is notified of the presence of the tribal police (later referred to as a "pirate" [Crowsong 2018, n.p. 19]), who, instead of helping her recover her lost crew member, tries to shoot down her ship. And although not much story is provided—especially considering the rich backstory provided online—S9 does open with an intriguing allusion to N. Scott Momaday's (Kiowa) classic *The Way to Rainy Mountain*.[32] Just as other science fiction comics above use their work to offer new twists on traditional stories, Crowsong uses his comic to provide the same treatment for one of the classic novels in Indigenous literature. The text of the novel accompanies artwork of an apparently injured astronaut struggling to make his way on a desolate planet. The final page of this opening vignette shows the astronaut coming upon a campfire with the narrator noting that "this is where creation began" (n.p. 4). What planet this is (Earth? A new planet with its own Indigenous population?) is unclear, as is its connection to the rest of the narrative. What is clear, however, is that once again we have an Indigenous writer rewriting a classic story into a narrative of technologically advanced Indigenous people

Figure 2.6. Richard Crowsong, *S9: Sequoyah 9*, vol. 1.

exploring the stars. And the backstory provided online explicitly notes
the politics of survivance, with Indigenous peoples rebuilding society
on Earth while simultaneously exploring the stars, suggesting that
space exploration (and technological development more generally)
need not come at the expense of environmental stewardship.

Finally, the clearest example of a science fiction survivance narrative—in terms of an "active sense of presence" (Vizenor 2009, 85)—is
Cole Pauls's (Tahltan) limited series *Dakwäkäda Warriors*.[33] Akin
to Jeffrey Veregge's work, Pauls's comic very clearly draws from the
aesthetic of the Indigenous peoples of the northwest: the ship piloted
by our protagonists is shaped like a raven's head and decorated with
stylized tribal line work, the map insert uses a traditional stylized
figure's face for the sun, and our heroes are dressed in space suits
decorated with stylized linework that includes animal heads for hel-
mets. In all three issues, the Dakwäkäda warriors Ts'ürk'i and A'ghay
battle Cyber Nàḻ and Space Kwäday Dän in outer space, protecting
Nän (Earth) from their nemeses' desire to "assimilate and colonize
your home" (Pauls 2017, n.p. 8). As such, *Dakwäkäda Warriors* is a
very clear statement against the machinations of settler colonization,
projected on a planetary scale. In what appears to be the far future,
then, Indigenous peoples must continue their fight against settler
colonization; having presumably attended to the issue on Earth, First
Nations warriors continue the fight to protect the planet, not unlike
what we have seen above in terms of environmental stewardship. In
volume 1, we see the warriors defeat their enemies by shooting down
their spaceship (drawn as a monstrous foot, perhaps suggesting that
they wish to "stamp out" Earth's inhabitants; Pauls 2016). Volume 2 has
the warriors protecting the Earth from their headquarters in Haines
Junction, Yukon Territory (Pauls's birthplace), a traditional log cabin
structure with an antenna atop a totem pole (Pauls 2017). In volume
3, the warriors return to space to defeat a giant, mechanized Mecha-
Bigfoot built to avenge their enemies' previous defeats (Pauls 2018).

However simple these plots seem to be, we must remember that
they are but the delivery for the books' true purpose: language preservation. In honor of having worked with "Vivian Smith, who has taught
him Southern Tutchone since he was in kindergarten," as well as "the
elders in his community, who shared their stories with him" (Vernet

2019, n.p.), Pauls composed these books to preserve and help teach Southern Tutchone. As he notes on the first page of volume 2: "There are two Southern Tutchone dialects; Champagne and Aishihik. The two language preservers I collaborated with, each speak one. Khâsha speaks the Champaign dialect and Vivian Smith speaks the Aishihik dialect. Collectively, the three of us incorporated the Southern Tutchone Language into this book" (Pauls 2017, n.p. i). Following this opening statement, Pauls provides a two-page glossary of Tutchone, as well as page references for each word. Volume 1 includes a one-page glossary at the end of the volume. Volume 3 includes a much longer two-page glossary (employing smaller print) and includes "a small amount of Tlingit words" that "were provided by my brother in law Blake Shaákoon Lepine."

By using a variety of common words seamlessly throughout the books (figure 2.7)—and by increasing both the number of words used as well as their frequency—his books work to gently increase his readers' useful vocabulary and assist in proper usage. It's also important to note that, in the illustration below, the characters are employing this language in conversation, showing the language to be living, rather than merely an artifact for academic study. And the implication is that the warriors—the technologically advanced individuals dressed in space suits in front of ships that allude to tribal artistry in animal representation—understand this language as well. In this regard, Pauls is looking toward the future in two ways: he is using the futuristic genre of science fiction to help build the future of the Southern Tutchone language. As such, Pauls is crafting a future that, like the rest of his Indigenous futurist peers, imagines a future populated—and in many ways led—by Indigenous peoples and additionally highlights a central component of Indigenous heritage and contemporary cultural preservation work. Here, perhaps, we see an example of the difference, noted by Elizabeth LaPensée (see Roanhorse et al. 2017, n.p.), between "decolonizing" and "sovereignty," between actively working against the machinery of settler-colonialism and the work of building Indigenous spaces out of Indigenous epistemologies, Indigenous aesthetics, and Indigenous culture (including language).

• • •

Figure 2.7. Cole Pauls, *Dakwäkāda Warriors*, vol. 3.

As the above works all demonstrate, science fiction narratives engaging in Indigenous futurisms are simultaneously familiar and defamiliarizing, using the familiar narrative form and tropes of science fiction to introduce their readers to the political, cultural, and aesthetic traditions of a variety of Indigenous peoples. Writers like Houseman, Storm, Sheyahshe, and Veregge all imagine future worlds where, despite the continuing efforts of the settler-colonial enterprise in North America today, Indigenous people not only survive but thrive: as stewards of this planet and the peoples who survive various kinds of destruction or as explores of the unknown. Other writers, like Starr, Crowsong, and Pauls (as well as Veregge), tackle the great unknown of science fiction narratives: outer space. However, while representation is certainly important—readers of all races benefit from seeing Indigenous peoples as scientists and explorers, leaders and heroes—it is not itself the goal. In starting to make up for decades of racist characterizations and stereotypes, the authors discussed above demonstrate that by expanding the canon to include Indigenous representation—both in terms of who is published and in what is allowed between the covers—we can witness the means by which genre conventions that have traditionally been used to disseminate the settler-colonial narrative can be more productively employed to upend that narrative. There is nothing inherently racist about exploration, about technological advancement, or about interacting with new cultures; Indigenous futurists are, at their core, showing us a new way to conceive of a future that leaves behind the biases and cultural destruction that has characterized settler-colonial states such as the United States and Canada. And as we will see in the following chapter, these same principles apply to the narratives of the past. In many ways, the past is still "unknown," whether we are talking about the erasure of certain stories from the official narrative or the continual uncovering of new information about the past. Just as creators of science fiction comics create possible worlds for their readers, so too do creators of historical comics. In both cases, Indigenous comic-book creators construct worlds that challenge what their readers know of our world, its past as well as its potential future.

CHAPTER 3

THE PAST IS PART OF THE PRESENT

Indigenous Historical Graphic Narratives

Even readers who have only a passing familiarity with Indigenous literature can probably speak to the importance of history to many Indigenous authors. Given the ubiquity of incorrect and harmful stereotypes that have come to be associated with Indigenous peoples and cultures, many Indigenous artists have used their works to more accurately represent their cultures and their pasts. In some cases, these efforts can take the form of representing tribal-specific histories that have been ignored by popular media or overlooked by the educational system. In other cases, these efforts work to correct existing narratives that have mischaracterized individual people, events, or cultures. As such, we can witness a clear educational impulse behind much of the historical fiction produced by Indigenous authors. And this impulse is no less apparent in the historical narratives being produced by those artists working in graphic narrative. In this regard, we can see historical graphic narratives produced by Indigenous artists as participating in what Georg Lukács (1983) identifies as one of the central concerns of historical fiction: the need for people "to comprehend their own existence as something historically conditioned, for them to see in history something which deeply affects their daily lives and immediately concerns them" (24). And as we will see below, many artists use their narratives to creatively connect the past to the present, demonstrating the continued importance of history to the lives of contemporary Indigenous peoples and cultures.

Although in some ways dated and oversimplified, Lukács's work provides a useful foundation for understanding the rise and importance of the genre of historical fiction (even if in general terms) while also highlighting some of the thematic and compositional aspects important to many writers of historical fiction, including the Indigenous writers whose work is analyzed in this chapter.[1] For instance, although Lukács (1983) himself is concerned with social class as opposed to racial identity, his identification of the importance of "increasing historical awareness of the decisive role played in human progress by the struggle of classes in history" (27) can easily be adapted to the study of race. This, of course, does not mean we should simply replace class with race in our concerns; rather, this is a call for a more thoroughly intersectional analysis of historical fiction than Lukács is concerned with.[2] As we will see in the works below, many Indigenous graphic novelists are using their work to highlight, reintroduce, or reframe various kinds of "struggle" engaged by Indigenous peoples and celebrating those individuals who have worked—and sometimes died—on behalf of their sovereign rights. These can be individual as well as communal struggles, personal as well as world-historical struggles. But perhaps most importantly, these struggles are not always faced by the historical figures who are central to the narratives.

One of Lukács's most important contributions to the study of historical fiction comes in his articulation of the role of the protagonist who serves as the link between the reader and the famous historical people and events. Following from his analysis of the novels of Sir Walter Scott—whose title character from *Waverley; Or, Tis Sixty Years Hence* (1814) provides the archetype of this character—Lukács (1983) comments on the "historically unknown, semihistorical or entirely non-historical persons" who "play this leading role" (38). It is through these relatively unknown (or invented) characters that readers come to witness the historical events and follow the actions of the individuals who populate our history books (or, in the case of many of the Indigenous figures discussed below, who have largely been relegated to footnotes or passing references in the historical record). However, whereas Scott—and those who followed in his footsteps, including authors like James Fenimore Cooper whose works contributed to the general mischaracterization of Indigenous peoples in the national imagination—drew on or created contemporaries of these historical figures and events, the Indigenous authors discussed below use characters contemporary with the reader, who serve to bring the reader into the historical narrative through various rhetorical means. In this regard, the works analyzed in this chapter engage in a more explicit means of what Lukács identifies as the "growing historical understanding for the problems of contemporary society" (231), by connecting these historical moments explicitly to the readers' present, thus forcing them to critically reevaluate what they know of their world. As we will see below, this move—connecting the reader to the past through an explicit connection to the reader's contemporary world, through protagonists who could be read as representing either the reader or people they would be familiar with—directly connects the contemporary world with the past while also actively humanizing the past for contemporary audiences, who may run the risk of thinking of the past as foreign or otherwise remote, thus missing its importance in their lives.

The connection between the artists' representation of historical moments—particularly traumatic moments, with repercussions still being addressed today—and the readers of these works is also a central concern of Kate Polak's study of historical graphic narratives. Where Lukács was more concerned with readers as a group, particularly in terms of social classes, Polak is interested in individual readers and their personal experiences.[3] As Polak (2017) argues, "Our representations of history have consequences, and those representations have the possibility of deploying empathy and identification in a variety of ways that make us see a situation through different points of view." The educational impulse I noted above is, in part, an effort not just to inform readers—particularly non-Indigenous readers[4]— about the history of Indigenous peoples, but also to encourage active changes in how we think about, represent, and ultimately treat Indigenous people. Polak alludes to this when she further notes that "too often the voices of the victims, the marginalized, and those subject to extreme oppression and violence are not included in the historical record" (15). However, I do not mean to suggest that any of the works discussed below are presentations of victimization—far from it. These works, like the works examined in other chapters, should be read as narrative acts of survivance. That said, we cannot ignore the victimization of Indigenous peoples and histories, particularly

by those people and institutions that have worked to craft the various manifestations of what we call the "historical record." Further,
while many of the works discussed below do in fact focus on "sites
of violence" that Polak notes authors of historical fiction operate at a
"relative distance from" (30), not all of these works focus on historical events associated with physical violence. In this regard, we should
perhaps intentionally misread Polak here or expand her concerns
to metonymically represent the larger acts of cultural violence that
come through erasure, stereotyping, or other rhetorical acts that have
removed Indigenous peoples from the historical record.

It is therefore important to remember that when we read about history, we are, of course, not witnessing the historical event itself or even
an unbiased, objective reporting of that history. As Polak (2017) comments about graphic narrative (as form), we could just as easily claim
about historical fiction (as genre): "Readers' awareness of the graphic
narrative as something *produced* is embedded in the form" (11). We
are reading a subjective retelling of the historical events, characters
based on historical people, and a narrative consciously constructed
for the benefit of the reader. As Polak argues, "Questioning how we
remember and narrate the past, as well as how we feel about it, has
become one of the crucial topics of the twenty-first century" (5). And
I would add to this by noting the increased importance of how the
histories of historically oppressed groups—including but certainly
not limited to Indigenous peoples—are remembered and narrated.
Historical narratives, then, are less representations of the past than
they are interpretations of the past; and as I will show below, the interpretations of the past analyzed in this chapter should be understood
as survivance narratives, embodying Gerald Vizenor's (2009) understanding of such work as "an active sense of presence over historical
absence, the dominance of cultural simulations, and manifest manners. Native survivance is a continuance of stories" (1). And in service
to that important work, these narratives—specifically chosen from a
much larger array of historical narratives produced by Indigenous
graphic narrative artists—also reflect Indigenous understandings of
time as well as representations of Indigenous pasts.

How we understand and represent time is central to how we understand and represent events from the past; more specifically, "history"

is not just a representation of the past but a reflection of how we understand our relationship with the past being represented. In sharp contrast to the Anglo-American tradition of historical fiction alluded to above in the discussion of Lukács—where the past is fundamentally different from the present, though certainly not unknowably so— much Indigenous historical fiction situates the past as fundamentally part of the present[5]; the past and present are intertwined, if not wholly coterminous. Many Indigenous creators employ a consciously non-chronological narrative, sometimes situating the narrative of the past within a narrative frame situated in the reader's present or bouncing back and forth between the past and the present. Whereas the former might suggest that the events of the past are central to understanding the present moment and the latter might draw direct parallels between the past and present (even suggesting that the historical periods may be coterminous), both techniques serve to reflect an understanding of time beyond a fixed, linear chronology; "history," in other words, is not some distant point on an unwavering timeline that we must study from afar but rather a foundation that can reside in both the individual and the culture to which they belong. In short, the past is not dead; it persists, even if temporarily forgotten. This persistence of the past is represented by the various Waverly figures alluded to above, who are here repurposed to serve as the common, everyday type through which we can understand history, while also demonstrating to the readers that they, too, can and should learn from and embody "history."

As such, these works all reflect—to varying degrees—nonlinear representations of time.[6] Whether we come to understand the flow of time as a spiral, following Abenaki scholar Lisa Brooks (2012)—who writes about "spiralic" time as "revolv[ing] through layers of generations, renewing itself with each new birth" (309)—or any of the other representations of the "achronology" that Laguna Pueblo artist and scholar Paula Gunn Allen (1986) notes "is the favored structuring device of American Indian novelists since N. Scott Momaday [Kiowa] selected it for organizing *House Made of Dawn*," what's important is that many Indigenous writers are consciously eschewing representing time linearly, in many cases for explicit socio-political purposes. As Lower Broule Sioux scholar and activist Nick Estes (2019) argues,

"Settler narratives use a linear conception of time to distance themselves from the horrific crimes committed against Indigenous peoples
and the land" (14). As such, Indigenous representations of nonlinear
time can be read as statements (on the level of formal narrative poetics) against the horrors of settler colonialism. This is especially the
case for works of historical fiction that challenge historical narratives
that are rooted in or otherwise support the master narrative of settler colonialism. Such narratives can be said to be working against
what Mark Rifkin (2017) calls "settler time," instead supporting an
"Indigenous temporal sovereignty" that "draws attention to the ways in
which settler superintendence of Native peoples imposes a particular
account of how time works" (26). In other words, we should read the
works discussed below—as well as other works of historical fiction
(graphic or otherwise) produced by Indigenous authors—as not just
retellings of a shared past but as arguments about how the past can
and should be understood: not as a distant point on a fixed timeline
but as an inherent component to our current lives. In other words,
the past is not just relevant to the present; it is *part of* the present.

I open this chapter with the analysis of two graphic novel series,
Métis writer Katherena Vermette's continuing series *A Girl Called
Echo* (illustrated by Scott B. Henderson and colored by Donovan
Yaciuk) and Norway House Cree writer David Alexander Robert-
son's limited series Tales from Big Spirit.[7] Unlike the other chapters
of this study, I will then turn to two works of nonfiction—Laguna
Pueblo writer and educator Dr. Lee Francis IV's and Tongva artist
Weshoyot Alvitre's *Ghost River: The Fall & Rise of the Conestoga* and
Yurok, Maida, and Achumawi writer Chag Lowry's *Soldiers Unknown*
(illustrated by Rashan Ekedal)—both of which engage in the same
aesthetic, narrative, and political work as the fictional series they are
paired with.

• • •

The various impulses noted above—such as a nonchronological
representation of time, narratives that demonstrate how the past is
inherently part of the present, and a clear educational impulse—are
all well-represented by Katherena Vermette's (Métis) ongoing series *A*

Girl Called Echo. Employing a protagonist who can be read squarely within the *Waverly* tradition, *Echo* follows the title character as she is transported back into select moments of historical importance that in various ways are explicitly connected to her life in the present. The series opens with a glimpse of the past: thirteen-year-old Echo Desjardins stands atop a rock overlooking Qu'appelle Valley in the Northwest Territories (now Saskatchewan) in 1814, although we learn a few pages later that this is a vivid dream after having fallen asleep in a history class covering a "Métis bison hunt" (Vermette 2017, 9). At least, we think it's only a dream, as her teacher awakens her for her next class. Later in the same book, however, after falling asleep again, Echo is transported back to that Métis camp where she interacts with the camp's inhabitants.[8] Echo thus becomes something of a time traveler, with each book bringing her back multiple times to a point in the past that has some relevance to her present life, in which she attends school as something of a quiet loner (wearing headphones, not joining with her classmates, giving one-word answers to questions about her day, etc.).

In the first volume of the series, *Pemmican Wars*, Echo learns about the daily life of the Métis in the early nineteenth century, which includes the domestic task of making pemmican as well as the outlawing of bison hunting on horseback, which will have a detrimental effect on their ability to feed themselves, all of which leads to the Battle at Seven Oaks between the Hudson's Bay Company and the North West Company (on whose side the Métis fought). And while the volume includes a useful "Timeline of the Pemmican Wars" (Vermette 2017, 45) for the reader interested in more of the historical events Echo lives through, learning this history is not necessarily the purpose of Echo's transportation in the narrative. Rather, her experiences with the nineteenth-century Métis first inform Echo about her cultural history and then inspire a sense of belonging to a community, a sense of belonging that she appeared to lack at the volume's opening. Whereas, at first, Echo seems to be avoiding talking to her mother,[9] after her adventures, she engages her mother in conversation, specifically asking about their family history (figure 3.1): "We're Métis, right?" (42). Echo clearly did not know much about her family history, and while she learns from her mother that "We are. Your grandpa was

Figure 3.1. Katherena Vermette, *A Girl Called Echo*, vol. 1.

very proud to be Métis," her mother also admits that "I don't really know much about it" (43) after being asked if she, too, is proud to be Métis. Note that, on this page, it's only in the first panel where we see Echo and her mother simultaneously; as they begin to talk about their heritage—a heritage Echo feels distant from—we see each character in their own panel, visually suggesting their distance from each other (at least on this topic). Then on the final page of the volume, we see Echo beginning to teach her mother about the Battle at Seven Oaks, which her mother has heard of but knows little about, thus suggesting just how much Echo has learned and how much closer she is to her mother as well as to her community.

Recalling that Echo noted to her history teacher that "I don't know anything about being Métis" (Vermette 2017, 37), we see that by the end of this first volume, Echo goes from being relatively ignorant about her cultural identity to speaking authoritatively about it, from learning about it (both in school and in her travels through time) to teaching about it, and from being the quiet kid who tries to hide to one seeking out conversation with her family about their history. The implication here is clear: the more Echo learns about her past, the more comfortable she becomes in the present. In this regard, "being Métis" is not a passive acceptance of a traditional identity but rather an active means of identifying herself, one which comes from a direct experience with her peoples' past. For Echo—and, arguably, for Vermette—"being Métis" is as much about understanding and embracing the past as it is about living in the present, even if (especially if?) the lives lived by the Métis in the early twenty-first century bear little resemblance to the lives lived by their nineteenth-century ancestors.

With each volume, Echo comes to learn more about Métis history and, in the process, becomes more involved with her own local Indigenous community. A history lesson about the Red River colony inspires Echo's travels back to the Red River settlement in 1869, where she witnesses Métis resistance to settler-colonial encroachment and the formation of the Métis provisional government to negotiate land rights with the Canadian government (figure 3.2). As we see in figure 3.2, her daydreaming in class is what brings her out of her time and into the past. And while she is not the only one who appears to dream their way out of the classroom, she is the only one who is transported

Figure 3.2. Katherena Vermette, *A Girl Called Echo*, vol. 2.

to the past, as opposed to the boy in front of her, who presumably is merely sleeping.

Whereas in the first volume she learned about the daily lives of the nineteenth-century Métis, now she is witness to one of the formative moments of Métis political history and the creation of the Métis List of Rights, which Vermette includes as an appendix to the volume. Echo is also present for the execution of Thomas Scott by the provisional government and the subsequent attack on the Métis by the Canadian armed forces, which included "looting, beating, and murdering" many peaceful and unarmed Métis. Echo (and the reader) learns that Louis Riel—Métis leader, politician, and revolutionary, famous for founding the province of Manitoba[10]—has fled with others to the United States just as she watches her new friend Benjamin leave with the rest of the community to find refuge "farther west" (Vermette 2018, 43). And while Echo witnesses such events that might suggest a fracturing of the Métis community—leaders separated from those they would serve; people being moved off of their lands by force—Echo herself becomes more involved in her local—especially her local Indigenous—community. We see Echo become friendly with her classmates and involved with her school's Indigenous Student Leadership program, signing up and later volunteering for the bake sale.[11] It is also after witnessing these historic events that Echo opens up and tells her guardian, "I miss my mom" (40). So as Echo comes to learn more about Métis history and the ways that the Métis have stood up for their rights against the encroaching settler-colonial Canadian state, so too does Echo metaphorically "stand up" and take a more active role in her life: she is more involved with her school and her peers, and she is more open about her feelings of loneliness and the pain of separation from her family.

The focus on Echo's personal development is continued in the third volume which—unlike the first two volumes—opens squarely in the present day of Echo's life. Whereas the first volume opens with an image of Echo in the past and the second with a split image showing a sleeping Echo (present) while dreaming of bison (past), the third volume situates Echo clearly in her present time, in a roundhouse meeting with her mother, who notes, "I am ready to go home" (Vermette 2020, 17). Their developing relationship—made stronger, as we will see below, at the end of the volume—parallels Echo's developing ability to travel back in time. Although seemingly unaware of its significance in the moment, Echo returns to the present while awake, instead of waking up as if from a dream. Echo's growing ability to control her gift is thus directly connected to her growing relationships with her family and her community, suggesting that the stronger her ties to the past become, the richer and more fulfilling her life becomes in the present.

Her first trip back in volume 3 is to March 1885, where a young Métis woman named Josephine brings her to a meeting run by Louis Riel and Gabriel Dumont, another Métis political leader born in the Red River community. After years of having their petitions and entreaties ignored by the Canadian government, the community decides to take up arms to defend their land claims in what will come to be known officially as the Northwest Rebellion but which the volume refers to as Northwest Resistance. (This seemingly small detail helps shift the focus of the event on the Métis resistance to settler-colonial encroachment rather than framing the incident in terms sympathetic to the Canadian government.) In her travels back throughout the volume, Echo witnesses the violent events of the resistance, leading to the surviving Métis having to once again leave their homes to find a safe place to rebuild their community. Riel himself surrenders to General Middleton, and the reader learns in the timeline included in the appendix that Riel was put on trial at Regina, found guilty of treason, and sentenced to death by hanging on November 16, 1885.[12] While one might be tempted to see this event—especially following those depicted in the first two volumes—as another setback for the Métis (and in a very real, political sense, it certainly was), the lesson here is not one of loss but of moving forward in the face of loss. The Métis are no closer to political independence and a recognition of their land claims by the Canadian government; however, they are also no less determined and no less sure in the inherent value of their community. Their continued strength is the lesson Echo seems to be learning from these trips, in addition to the finer details of the history of her people.

This lesson Echo learns about her people is strengthened by what she is learning about herself (such as her own strength in the face of difficulties) and is cemented by what she is learning about her own family history. Early in the third volume, Echo is reintroduced to Benjamin, whom she met in the second volume, as Josephine's father, thus connecting her various trips back in time to one another. At the end of the volume, Echo learns that Benjamin and Josephine are relatives: after her conversation with Echo in the last volume, Echo's mother gets a genealogy chart made, and in addition to the chart, her mother is provided with pictures (figure 3.3). Remembering figure 3.1 above, we see in figure 3.3 the way that Echo and her mother are now working together, both of them handling and viewing the family photos and genealogy.

The reader learns along with Echo that Benjamin and Josephine are direct ancestors and that Benjamin survived both resistances (which, admittedly, Echo already knew from her travels back in time). This revelation serves two purposes within the narrative, one more obvious than the other. First, Echo is not being transported back in time randomly but is traveling to times and places where she can directly interact with her ancestors. That this realization comes in the volume where she is reunited with her mother strengthens the readers' understanding of the importance of family, both immediate and ancestral, for Echo (and, as such, for the Métis community she belongs to). Second, it is also important that this revelation comes at this specific point in the narrative.

This scene between Echo and her mother is continued in the following volume, where Echo's mother recounts family stories about Josephine, who was the first in their family to move to the city. Following this conversation—and the realization that the people who have served as guides to her travels in the past are direct relatives— Echo wills herself to travel to the past by noting "I want to go back to Josephine" (Vermette 2021, 4). Starting in volume 4, Echo is able to travel back in time at will and does so again later in the volume when she learns that the Métis community at Ste. Madeleine was "burned to the ground" in 1939. Earlier in the volume, Echo learns that was where Benjamin, Josephine, and their community were headed after Riel's execution in 1885. Echo visits the Métis community in 1939 and is told by an older Josephine that "I know that our people will survive because you have survived, and you are strong and well, and will do so many great things." Just as Echo has been gaining strength

Figure 3.3. Katherena Vermette, *A Girl Called Echo*, vol. 3.

Figure 3.4. Katherena Vermette, *A Girl Called Echo*, vol. 4.

from her visits to the past, so too has the Métis community from the past gained strength by her visits. In other words, whereas the first few volumes suggest that Echo is drawing strength from the past, the fourth volume makes clear that the relationship between the present and past is mutually beneficial. The benefits of community development do not run merely along strictly chronological lines, with Echo's travels making clear the past's influence on the present. The present (the future, for the Métis of the past) also directly strengthens those in the past, who know that their community will survive the various political setbacks and violent suppressions in some form. Upon returning to her own time, Echo learns from her mother that, since the events of 1939, "we've won most of our land-claim cases since then, over the years" (41) and is reminded by her mother that she carries the strength of the whole Métis community—past and present—with her in her endeavors. In the final image of the volume (figure 3.4), Echo is shown graduating from middle school, symbolizing her own growth and development as an individual. Behind her are her contemporary family members, and behind them is the Métis community from the past. Separating those in the present from those in the past is the Métis flag, connecting them by cultural history, even though they are separated by time. The message is clear: the past and the present are part of one, simultaneous community.

· · ·

The narrative tactic of using sleep as a means of traveling to the past has also been employed in *The Ballad of Nancy April—Shawnadithit*, written by David Alexander Robertson (Norway House Cree) and illustrated by Scott B. Henderson, who also illustrates *A Girl Called Echo*.[13] Like the rest of the Tales from Big Spirit books, *The Ballad of Nancy April—Shawnadithit* teaches readers about an important figure from Canadian First Nations history.[14] While cutting through the woods on a shortcut home, young Jessie breaks her necklace before lying down to rest; after falling asleep, she is transported back to the past, first as "the wind," where she "hears the Beothuk people raise their prayers" as well as their "oral histories [that] tell of [how] the white-skinned ones are unstoppable" (Robertson 2014a, 5). Jessie then witnesses the moment of first contact in the late fifteenth century in what is now called Newfoundland, followed by the European settler-colonists establishing their society "over the next centuries" (11). She then stops in the early nineteenth century, where she witnesses the birth of Shawnadithit, born into a time when the numbers of Beothuk have dwindled and "the birth of a young one is cause for great celebration" (12). However, as the reader learns later, Shawnadithit will become known as "the last Beothuk" after the slaughter of her people by the European settler-colonists, as well as the forced assimilation of the few who remain, including Shawnadithit, who is later given the name Nancy April.

Eventually "taken into the care of William Cormack" (Robertson 2014a, 28), founder of the Beothuk Institute, Shawnadithit shares her stories and artwork with Cormack, assisting in preserving what they could of traditional Beothuk knowledge. In this way, one could argue that Shawnadithit—through her work—survives into the present. However, Robertson brings her into the present much more explicitly and much more personally. After Shawnadithit dies, the narrative concludes with the second half of the frame tale; Jessie awakens and returns to her family. Concerned about her broken necklace, her father notes that she's already wearing one, an unfamiliar one. When asked who gave it to her, Jessie replies, "it was a gift" (30), remembering that she was witness to the history of the Beothuk generally and the life of Shawnadithit specifically (figure 3.5).

As Jessie stands in the grass, she remembers Shawnadithit, who wore that same necklace at the end of her life. The insert panels on the left of the page suggest that Shawnadithit is there with Jessie, who rubs her eyes to make sure she is seeing things clearly. Shawnadithit—both as an individual and as an embodiment of the cultural knowledge she recorded for future generations—is still part of the present, living within the person of Jessie, who herself represents the next generation of Indigenous youth.

The remainder of the Tales from Big Spirit books all work in a similar fashion: the reader learns about an important (and oftentimes understudied[15]) Indigenous historical figure, whose life is connected to the present by the use of some kind of frame narrative. Sleep is again used in *The Land of Os—John Ramsay*: in a dream, young Richard

Figure 3.5. David Alexander Robertson, *The Ballad of Nancy April—Shawnadithit*.

meets an unidentified man who feeds him before instructing him to bring a can of white paint with him on his school trip the following day. On this field trip, Richard and his classmates learn about John Ramsay from his granddaughter, who narrates to the class a short history of Ramsay's founding of Os, his work assisting Icelandic settlers even as he needed to protect that land against those who would take it from him and whose efforts helped some of the Sandy Bar community survive smallpox. After his death, Ramsay appeared in a dream by Trausti Vigfusson, Icelandic settler who now lives on the land where Ramsay's first wife, Betsey, was buried; Trausti was tasked with rebuilding the fence that protected her grave so that "her resting place can't be lost and forgotten" (Robertson 2014b, 27). At the close of the narrative frame, Richard realizes that all his classmates had the same dream and that they were supposed to repaint the worn fence. As with Jessie, Richard has a direct, personal interaction with a historical figure who leaves some mark—for the former, a necklace; for the latter, a painted fence—in the present as a material reminder of their lives and legacies. And in both cases, these material tokens symbolize the continued influence these individuals have on their communities: just as Shawnadithit left behind stories and maps that helped preserve Beothuk cultural knowledge into the present, Ramsay built a memorial site to a beloved spouse, the upkeep of which continues the tradition of community support Ramsay established in Os.

Akin to *The Land of Os—John Ramsay*, *The Scout—Tommy Prince* employs an individual who tells the story of the title character: Sergeant Tommy Prince, from the Brokenhead Ojibwe Nation, who served in the Canadian Army during World War II and the Korean War while becoming Canada's most decorated First Nations soldier (Robertson 2014f). Similar to how John Ramsay appeared to Richard (and his classmates) in a dream, the spirit of Tommy Prince (1915–1977) is standing at his memorial in Winnipeg when Pamela comes by while chasing down a baseball. Unaware of whom she was speaking with, Pamela listens to the friendly soldier as he relates to her his life: attending the Elkhorn Residential School, serving honorably in the Canadian Army in one of their elite special-forces units, and later saving the life of a drowning man after his honorable discharge (figure 3.6).

Figure 3.6. David Alexander Robertson, *The Scout—Tommy Prince*.

Prince's continued presence in the world is noted on the final page of the book in two related ways. First, Pamela notes that she's "gonna tell my friends about him" (Robertson 2014f, 30), keeping alive the story that the physical monument can allude to but not articulate (not unlike the grave at Os). But just as importantly, Prince himself is still meaningfully in the world, even if in a noncorporeal way—sharing his story with Indigenous children, as suggested by the final panel of the narrative where the reader clearly sees that the face on the memorial is the face of the man Pamela spoke with (and who mysteriously disappears at the end of his tale). The suggestion here is that the values Prince embodied—bravery, support of his community, and selflessness—remain alive among Canada's First Nations populations. This narrative device is repeated—albeit with a twist—in *The Rebel—Gabriel Dumont* when students use a secret time machine located in the school's basement to bring to the present Gabriel Dumont, the Métis leader also briefly discussed in *A Girl Called Echo*. Brought to the present primarily because the students want to "make history fun" as they "don't like text books [*sic*]" (Robertson 2014e, 3), Dumont teaches the students about the events leading up to the May 9, 1885 Battle of Batoche, part of the Northwest Resistance.

The remaining books in the series don't necessarily involve time travel—either people from the present traveling to the past or those from the past appearing in the present—but they do still erase the temporal boundaries to highlight the ways that the past still lives in the present. For instance, in *The Poet—Pauline Johnson*, the nerves of elementary school student Kathy toward reading her poetry aloud to her classmates is visually paralleled by Pauline Johnson's nerves when reading at her friend's literary event (Robertson 2014d). Popularly known as the "Mohawk Princess," Johnson became an in-demand poet, public speaker, and writer (whose poetry is still regularly taught in the classroom at schools and universities located in traditional Haudenosaunee lands). Drawing inspiration from Johnson, Kathy performs to the delight of her classmates. Although not traveling through time, Johnson's presence lives on in all the young Indigenous girls who use the arts to find their voice. Literature is again used in *The Chief—Mistahimaskwa* when Sarah opens her biography of the nineteenth-century Cree chief and is then able to witness the major

Figure 3.7. David Alexander Robertson, *The Chief—Mistahimaskwa.*

events of his life (Robertson 2016). In both cases, the students learn valuable lessons from these important historical figures, whose lives are brought into the present by the power of language, whether this is the persistence of Johnson's poetic achievements or the symbolism of the magic book that quite literally gives Kathy a close-up view of the past (figure 3.7). Upon opening the book, the historical figure is brought to life for the reader, who then offers the book to an unenthusiastic classmate to help them learn presumably because there is more to this particular book than just the words on the page.

The Peacemaker—Thanadelthur also employs the power of language to connect the past to the present. Just as Kathy overcomes her fears of public speaking, so too does Cole, who is assigned a presentation on an important figure from First Nations history as punishment. Admitting to his older sister that he does not know about any historical figures he could present on and, even if he did, he's too nervous to speak in front of his classmates, his sister tells him the story of Thanadelthur, an eighteenth-century Cree woman who negotiated peace between the Cree and the Dene. Inspired both by Thanadelthur's bravery as well as the importance of public speaking that she embodied, Cole gives a presentation about her to his class the following day (Robertson 2014c).[16]

● ● ●

Although this chapter—indeed, this whole book—focuses on fiction, I would be remiss if I did not spend some time discussing a couple of the excellent nonfiction works that, similar to the fictional narratives discussed above, insist upon the persistence of the past into the present. And given the ubiquitous presence of historical figures in the fictional narratives discussed above (even if some of those narratives use fictional frames to bookend otherwise nonfictional narratives), it may be worthwhile to simply ignore the distinction between fiction and nonfiction to otherwise focus on narrative especially as many of the nonfiction narratives work with the same educational impulse as the books discussed above (even as they lack some of the additional materials that Highwater Press includes for many of their publications).

As readers are well aware, narrative—as a means of communication—does not favor either fiction or nonfiction and is as suitable for the relation of events that never occurred as it is for those that are historically verifiable.[17] And as historian Hayden White (1987) reminds us, "a discourse [here including but not exclusive to narrative[18]] is regarded as an apparatus for the production of meaning rather than as only a vehicle for the transmission of information about an extrinsic referent" (42). That is to say, a narrative is not merely a summary of the events of the story being told; or, to use terminology common among narrative theorists, the story (the events being narrated) is not the same as the discourse (the manipulation of those events into a narrative). Whether the story is nonfictional, fictional, or some combination of the two, the events are manipulated into a narrative, which gives shape to those events but also assigns meaning to those events. Along these lines, White asks, "Has any historical narrative ever been written that was not informed not only by moral awareness but specifically by the moral authority of the narrator?" (21). Here, White asks his readers to recognize that historical narratives always serve not only a larger goal but specifically a moral one, one that assigns moral value to the events. Put simply, narrative discourses of events (as opposed to chronicles of those events) assign the distinction between "right" and "wrong"; historical narratives are not just accounts of events but, moreover, arguments about how their readers should interpret those events. And as we have seen in the fictional historical narratives discussed above, the authors of nonfictional historical narratives use their works to argue explicitly that the past can and should be understood as inherently part of our current lives. The past is *part of* the present.

Perhaps the best example of such a work in comics is *Ghost River: The Fall & Rise of the Conestoga*, written by Dr. Lee Francis IV (Laguna Pueblo) with art by Weshoyot Alvitre (Tongva) and edited by Will Fenton. I am not claiming that this text is a more thoroughly engaging read than others (though, it certainly is engaging) or that its manipulation of narrative devices outpaces its peers; rather, my estimation of it as the "best" place to begin has everything to do with the larger work accompanying this book, both online and in physical form at the Library Company of Philadelphia, which commissioned this book. In addition to a wonderful graphic novel, this project includes a rich variety of online contextual materials, including lesson plans for teaching this book, essays providing various kinds of context for this book, and a digital record of historical artifacts that readers can use to better understand the historical events recounted in the book. Additionally, the Library Company of Philadelphia displayed (until April 2020) a rich exhibit tied to this book, including such materials as Alvitre's hand-painted artwork for the graphic novel, various historical materials from the period, and a wampum belt created by Wampanoag artist Elizabeth James-Perry, which as we will see below is central to the graphic novel's representation of time. Given the rich mosaic of materials associated with this book—many of which remain curated online, for curious readers as well as faculty who wish to teach this book in their classes—*Ghost River* is more rooted in the history it conveys than most other historical narratives. And as such, we can use it as a paradigmatic example of how nonfictional historical narratives can perform the same work as their fictional counterparts.

Recounting the murder of twenty Conestoga individuals by the so-called "Paxton Boys" in 1763, *Ghost River* works much in the same way as *A Girl Called Echo* and the Tales from Big Spirit series: an important story about Indigenous people from the past is retold for a contemporary audience and told in such a way so as to suggest the continued importance of that story and the lessons learned from it for those in the present.[19] Unlike the other books noted above, however, *Ghost River* opens much further in the past, reaching back to "the beginning of our knowledge of time" (Francis 2019, 12) before quickly moving through the sixteenth through the eighteenth centuries before coming to December 1763, where the readers learn that the Conestoga have been murdered by witnessing a conversation taking place among the Lenape people on Province Island. In this way, Francis notes to his readers that this event was newsworthy among the local Indigenous populations just as it was among the settler-colonial populations in Pennsylvania.[20] The narrative then jumps in time to December 2013, where contemporary Conestoga people participate in the "Reading of the Names" (24), an event where the names of the murdered Conestoga are spoken aloud and remembered by their descendants. In this way, Francis's story and Alvitre's artwork subtly suggest to the reader that the ancestors from the past remain with their descendants in the future: their story remains told (even if, until now, largely among the Conestoga themselves), and their names are remembered. And by moving around in time—breaking the linear conception of time in ways similar to the fictional narratives discussed above—*Ghost River* uses its narrative form to suggest that the past is interwoven in the present, that the contemporary Conestoga live with their ancestors much in the same way that Echo doesn't just "visit" her ancestors, given that they remain with her in the present.

In addition to the narrative, the artwork also subtly connects the present to the past, demonstrating their contiguity. Pages 32–33 provide a two-page spread depicting the creation of a wampum belt, a piece of traditional craft work that, in addition to its inherent aesthetic value, has often been used to symbolize an agreement between two

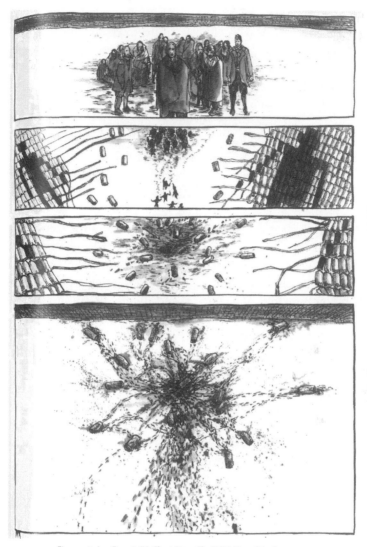

Figure 3.8. Lee Francis IV, *Ghost River: The Fall & Rise of the Conestoga*.

parties while telling the story of that agreement in the design of the bead work. This belt reappears at multiple points in the narrative, including following the massacre (figure 3.8). The reader is presented with an image of the Conestoga just prior to their murder. The murder is then shown in the second panel, which is framed by the wampum belt now torn in half, symbolizing the broken agreement between the Conestoga and the settler-colonists. In the third and fourth panels, the bodies of the murdered Conestoga are replaced by the bloodied beads of the wampum belt, lying in the snow amid the footprints of the now-dead people. The belt—like the peace between the two groups—has been violently destroyed.

However, that peace—and the wampum belt that symbolizes it— can be remade. Even though the murdered Conestoga cannot return to their community, those who survive can rebuild the peace and the sense of community between peoples. The final image of the wampum belt appears near the close of the narrative, in a section dated August 14, 2018. The belt has been mended (or perhaps remade), showing the peace between the settler-colonial people and the Conestoga, following a page where the narrator notes, "The stories we tell of the Conestoga . . . give us understanding of how a people lived and endured" (Francis 2019, 64). The Conestoga—despite the attempts by the Paxton Boys to annihilate them and attempt to gain support for further efforts—remain in the area and have lived to tell their stories. And those stories—as well as the events such as the "Reading of the Names"—are part of the larger efforts to create that lasting peace. In fact, we should remember that the individual Conestoga who were murdered are only all named during the "Reading of the Names"; that is to say, their identities are given not during the period in which they lived but in the contemporary world of today's reader. This should be read as a subtle nod to their continued existence as individuals, just as the Conestoga as a people continue to exist today. This could be the reason for the novel's seemingly awkward subtitle: the common expression "rise and fall" is here inverted, suggesting that what fol- lows is not a story about those who have fallen but rather those who have risen. This is not a story about those who died but about those who remain, and that symbolically includes the twenty Conestoga who were murdered.

In his book *Soldiers Unknown*, Chag Lowry (Yurok, Maidu, and Achumawi) uses a similar technique to collapse the time between the past and the present, thus showing that the past remains in the pres- ent, that it is a part of who we are today. "Based on the true-life experi- ences of Yurok Native American men from northwestern California during World War One," *Soldiers Unknown* tells the story of three cousins who took part in "the American military's largest engagement of the Great War . . . the Meuse-Argonne offensive" (Lowry 2019, 6) in 1918. And as we have seen with the various historical narratives discussed above, this important story is framed by (and interspersed with) a contemporary story: Wallace, himself a veteran of the US Marine Corps (his shoulder tattoo is prominently displayed on page 108), prepares for participation in a Yurok ceremony where he will sing and wear the *play-gok*, which the reader learns is a piece of headgear worn during a ceremony. Wallace learns that his *play-gok* was made by his great-grandfather Charley, who was "chosen to be the center-man" (8) in this ceremony, after which he and his relations Morek and Thomas were drafted to serve during WWI. While much of the book deals with the various kinds of pain and loss that were suffered by soldiers during and after war (including Morek's death, the death of Thomas's father while he was away, and Charley's difficulty in returning to life at home after the horrors of war), the frame narrative centered on Wallace is focused more on the survivance of Indigenous peoples and their traditions. Although prohibited from participating in the ceremony due to his participation in the war, Charley turned his attention to (among other efforts) making "regalia for others to use and wear" (113).

This piece of regalia, the colorful *play-gok* Wallace wears on his head at the end of the book, is used similarly to the wampum belt in *Ghost Dance*. Appearing at various points of the narrative, the *play-gok* is prominently displayed in both the present narrative focused on Wallace and the past narrative focused on Charley. Perhaps more importantly, it is also the opening image on the first page, with the four panels appearing to pull back the camera to give increasingly larger views of this important cultural artifact, as well as the final image of the book, appearing on the last page after the afterword. That is to say, in addition to tying together the past and present narratives recounted in the book, the *play-gok* also frames the book, highlighting its importance to the narrative. Perhaps its most important symbolic usage—at least for the purposes of my reading—comes on pages 103–4 (Lowry 2019). Injured by a bullet and lying in the ruins of a church, Charley has a vision of a woman in traditional clothing

Figure 3.9. Chag Lowry, *Soldiers Unknown*.

bringing him a basket. Working in opposition to the imagery of the first page of the novel, the panels on page 103 show an increasingly close up view of the basket, whose design work is identical to the *play-gok* that Wallace wears on the following page (figure 3.9).

The reader knows that this *play-gok* is the same as the one Charley made nearly one hundred years ago and, as such, works as a physical artifact tying together Charley and Wallace as well as the past and the present. By witnessing the older generation tying it to the head of the younger generation, the reader sees how this artifact is meant to be passed down, to connect generations (not unlike the Métis flag seen above). As we learn at the end of the novel, "It took [Charley] over fifty years to make the *play-gok*" Wallace is going to wear, suggesting its personal value for Charley and its cultural value for the Yurok, as a physical piece of cultural history that ties together multiple generations of Yurok. And so that this point isn't lost on the reader, the elder who tells this story to Wallace explicitly notes, "Our ancestors are always with us" (Lowry 2019, 113), a point emphasized by the continued presence (and use) of the *play-gok* and the continuation of the ceremony for which it is used (and which closes the narrative on a two-page display).

• • •

As the various narratives discussed above demonstrate, many Indigenous graphic novelists who work with historical narratives do so—at least in part—to highlight the continued importance of the past in the lives of contemporary Indigenous peoples. With its accompanying additional materials—especially those related to teaching—series like Tales from Big Spirit show the value of such works in the teaching of Indigenous history, a history that scholar-activists, such as Nick Estes, suggest is not relegated to the past. Remembering that "settler narratives use a linear conception of time to distance themselves from the horrific crimes committed against Indigenous peoples and the land" (Estes 2019, 14), we should read such works as those discussed above as reminders that the past is always part of the present. And while Estes here focuses on the horrific crimes perpetrated against Indigenous peoples, many of the above narratives also highlight the positive cultural survivance of Indigenous peoples and traditions. Further, continuing series like *A Girl Called Echo* demonstrate the popular interest among readers for stories that engage history in compelling ways, especially for younger readers. As such, Indigenous historical comics and graphic novels are becoming an increasingly sought-after product for general readers and students alike. And just as many of the creators discussed in this chapter employ what many (especially non-Indigenous) readers may see as an "experimental" approach to time, the creators in the next and final chapter explicitly engage in the creation of experimental narratives, experimenting with aspects of composition and storytelling that provide new ways to critique the politics of settler colonialism.

CHAPTER 4

PUSHING THE BOUNDARIES OF REPRESENTATION

Indigenous Experimental Graphic Narrative

If it's the case that Indigenous-authored comics and graphic novels have gone largely unnoticed by the scholarly community, then it is even more so the case that "experimental" works by such authors have failed to receive the scholarly attention that they deserve. And I argue this is the case for two reasons. First, "experimental" comics themselves are understudied texts in the field of comic-book studies.[1] In some cases, these works may be difficult to classify. How, for instance, does one classify a work like Joshua W. Cotter's (2009) *Driven by Lemons*? At times there seems to be a first-person narrator, but this narrative voice is not consistent throughout the text (figure 4.1). At times, the narrative is conveyed through images only (much like the "wordless novels" of Frans Masereel and Lynd Ward), while, at others, the pages contain (seemingly) random shapes and patterns, at times employing different artistic styles. And throughout, "characters" are drawn with varying degrees of realistic representation (some are anthropomorphized shapes), and dialog consists of apparent non sequiturs. The experimental nature of the narrative and representation seems only highlighted by the use of what appear to be traditional panels, with each page employing a three-by-four grid that doesn't change, suggesting no use of the gutter to transmit meaning and with no attempt made for the panel to convey narrative information.

In other cases, these works may be difficult to obtain; mainstream publishers are far less likely to produce and distribute a work that has no obvious (and successful) parallel on the market. Take, for instance, Chris Ware's (2012) work *Building Stories*, a boxed collection of "14 distinctively discrete Books, Booklets, Magazines, Newspapers, and

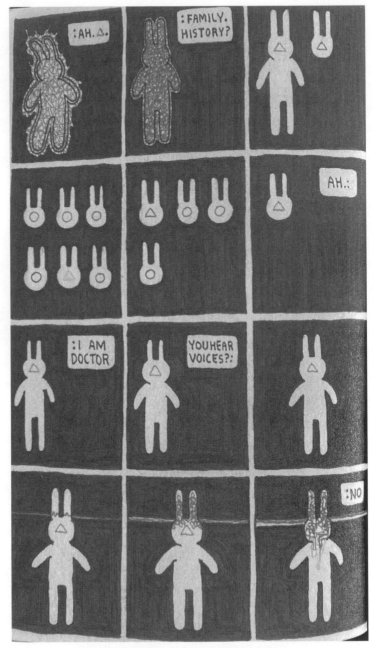

Figure 4.1. Joshua W. Cotter, *Driven by Lemons*.

Pamphlets" (box set bottom cover). These various individual—albeit multiply linked—stories all contribute pieces to a much larger narrative and, as such, can be read as a "graphic novel." However, as my parenthetical citation also suggests, this work is physically much different from other graphic novels; the fourteen pieces are collected in a large (11.7 × 1.9 × 16.7 inches) box, with no instruction on how—or in which order—to read them, unlike most graphic novels that are meant to be read by flipping the pages one at a time (as one would read most of the individual pieces from *Building Stories*). Although eventually published in 2012 by Pantheon Books, Ware originally pitched a similar idea to Eclipse Comics in 1987, who passed on the project. And while there are certainly many reasons for those decisions, one factor that we must take into consideration is that in the years between the rejection from Eclipse and the approval from Pantheon (in 2006) was Ware's growing recognition as a graphic novelist, launched by his being the first comic-book artist to win a major UK publishing award, as the 2001 winner of the Guardian First Book Award for *Jimmy Corrigan: The Smartest Kid on Earth*.[2] If nothing else, one has more leeway in publishing nontraditional work when one has been lauded for past achievements.

In a similar vein, the second reason why experimental comics by Indigenous creators have not been more thoroughly studied is certainly due to the larger lack of attention paid to experimental narratives by Indigenous artists. The vast majority of scholarship on Indigenous literature focuses on reading the literature as a product of Indigenous culture, retelling traditional stories for a modern audience and/or documenting the lives of Indigenous peoples, whether in a historical setting or a contemporary one. And while many scholars and writers have dismissed the label "Native American Renaissance" as referring more to the academy's acceptance of Indigenous authors into the canon than any concerted effort by Indigenous authors to produce "literary" works, much of the scholarship on Indigenous literature continues to focus on reading those works (not wrongly, I should note) as expressions of tribal histories, identities, and cultural practices. While it is certainly the case that a great many Indigenous artists use their works to engage with and disseminate aspects of their cultural heritage—and this is no less so the case with the authors discussed below—it is equally the case that oftentimes the formal qualities of the narrative are ignored in favor of an explication of the thematic aspects of the texts.[3] Even when the work of Indigenous authors is rightly celebrated for its "experimental" nature, it's common for critics either to call something experimental because it mixes genres or to simply note (with little or no development) that a work *is* experimental before moving on. For instance, in her analysis of Leslie Marmon Silko's (Laguna Pueblo) *Storyteller* (1981), Cynthia Carsten (2006) notes: Silko "experiments with multiple genres—fiction, poetry, historical narrative, and memoir—within a single work. In addition, Silko subverts the Euro-American aesthetic expectations of temporal continuity and chronology of plot" (107). Cartsen later quickly characterizes Silko's *Sacred Water* (1993) as "experimental" due to its combination of "pairing narratives with visual images" (125n25). Richard Stock (2016), in his analysis of Louise Erdrich's (Turtle Mountain Chippewa) *Love Medicine* (1984), notes that Erdrich's place as a postmodern experimental writer "seems easy to prove" (120) before comparing Erdrich to such established (white, male) postmodernists as Thomas Pynchon and David Foster Wallace.[4] In either case, the literary experimentation is not the primary focus of the analysis and, at times, seems to be shorthand for describing a work that does not fall neatly into a preexisting literary-critical category (at least as such categories have been determined by Western, Euro-American academic communities).

At this point, then, it would be helpful to posit a working definition of "experimental" that is not merely an articulation of the mixing of genres or—even worse—equates "experimental" with "postmodern." In their "Introduction" in *The Routledge Companion to Experimental Literature*, Joe Bray, Alison Gibbons, and Brian McHale (2012) eschew any proscriptive definition of "experimental," claiming instead, "The one feature that *all* literary experiments share is their commitment to raising fundamental questions about the very nature of verbal art itself. What *is* literature, and what could it be? What are its functions, its limitations, its possibilities?" (1). With their emphasis on "verbal art," however, their definition (perhaps unintentionally) hints at one of the problems in defining an experimental graphic narrative, one noted by Hillary Chute in her contribution to the volume. Opening

the chapter "Graphic Narrative," Chute (2012) notes, "In the historically relative sense of the term, the medium of comics has always
been experimental" (407). So how, then, do we define experiments
within a medium that—for many scholars and readers alike—is
already defined as experimental? Chute then provides an answer by
taking her definition of "experimental" from Marianne DeKoven's
scholarship on Gertrude Stein: a text is experimental when it causes
"the obstruction of normal reading" (DeKoven qtd. in Chute 2012,
407).[5] Chute further defines comics as "a non-transparent form that
always shows its seams, calling attention to its construction" (407).
And in this regard, we might say that the works discussed below not
only call attention to their construction (and deconstruction, as we
will see with Yahgulanaas) but also (to varying degrees) lay bare the
site of construction for the reader. Because merely calling attention
to the constructed nature of comics is not enough to be experimental,
many comics artists will also employ new tools in the construction (as
we will see with eelonqa K. harris [whose name is lowercase]). Such
efforts are not performed solely for the sake of experimentation; each
of the experiments is designed specifically to bring the reader into the
act of meaning making generally and, in some cases, the construction
of the final artistic product; such work also carries immense cultural
value for the artists, whose work is as much a political statement as
it is an aesthetic one.

   As such, any discussion of the formal experimentation of non-
white artists must work in tandem with an articulation of the political
significance of such work, even if that work is not explicitly (or obviously) political. Beth Berila (2005) perfectly articulates what is really
at stake when we apply a label such as "experimental" to non-white
authors; I quote her here at length:

   One of the key issues this body of works raises is, of course,
   how experimental multiethnic literature gets defined. In the
   larger field of literary studies, experimental writing often
   breaks conventional form, disrupts linear narrative and temporal sequence, mixes mediums and genres, shifts between
   characters' perspectives and voices, and self-reflexively comments on its form. Many of these aesthetic traits are also

found in experimental multiethnic literature, but the latter often questions the degree to which these characteristics are "experimental" since what "breaks" conventional form depends on how conventional form itself is defined, a definition which is shaped by historic and contemporary racial politics . . . . Multiethnic experimental literature often reveals how meaning production is deeply embedded in the shifting categories of race, ethnicity, gender, sexuality, and nation. (32)

When categorizing the work of non-white authors as "experimental," it's not enough to simply identify a set of genre-based and/or genre-breaking devices, particularly when those authors write from and within non-Western/non-Euro-American traditions (even if the final product does fall within the Western notion of "graphic narrative"). To return to the case of Silko, what many readers unfamiliar with Laguna Pueblo storytelling might read as "experimental" in her novel *Ceremony* (1977), readers from the Laguna Pueblo community (or those familiar with the narrative conventions of that community) might read as "traditional," an adjective that would appear to be at odds with "experimental." In different ways, the experimental texts discussed below comment on issues of identity (even if not always focused on race), and when they do engage in racial politics, they do so through the use of an experimental formal device. That is to say, in some cases, the formal experimentation highlights racial politics or brings to the foreground the issue of racial representation. In this regard, some aspects of the work may be thoroughly "traditional"—by which I mean "standard for graphic novels" as well as "drawn from the author's cultural heritage"—while others are innovative.

In one respect then, "experimental" must be something (relatively) new, and the works I will discuss below are in some way (at the time of this writing) unique, engaged in a kind of work that is not (yet) commonplace among comic-book artists. However, these works also all play (to some degree) with familiar graphic-narrative conventions, which are readily identifiable by anyone with a passing familiarity with comics and graphic novels. And while discussing these works with others would provide a different (and just as valuable) interpretive framework, I want the focus here to be on their formal experimentations and why those experimentations matter. Because these works are not just new ways of looking at potentially familiar plots and characters; as Berila notes, the experimentation is centrally concerned with exploring the process of meaning making, specifically a racially embodied understanding of meaning making. That is to say, these texts employ experimental qualities not simply for the sake of formal experimentation but also to force the reader to grapple with important cultural or political issues that might otherwise be much easier to ignore.

This final chapter will provide an in-depth analysis of the work of two experimental graphic novelists: Haida artist and activist Michael Nicoll Yahgulanaas and the northwest tribal writer and educator who publishes under the pen name eelonqa K. harris. Both writers have published multiple books that explore new means of composing art that fall under the larger umbrella of comics artistry while simultaneously engaging in the political work of their more mainstream contemporaries.

● ● ●

One such graphic novelist whose work develops a noteworthy type of formal experimentation to raise an important cultural issue is Michael Nicoll Yahgulanaas (Haida). A descendant of noted Haida artists Isabella and Charles Edenshaw—who worked in a variety of media, including basketry, woodcarving, jewelry, and painting—Yahgulanaas is perhaps most well known as both a visual and an installation artist, whose works have been exhibited across the globe; Yahgulanaas has had work commissioned by the British Museum (2010) and the Winter Olympics Organizing Committee (2010), among many others. Some of his more popular works are his installation pieces made out of reclaimed cars; these include such works as *Trans Am Totem* (2015), which stacks five cars atop a large tree stump, and *Pedal to the Meddle* (2007), a Pontiac Firefly whose hood has been painted with Haida-inspired designs. As Nicola Levell (2016) notes in her study of Yahgulanaas, *The Seriousness of Play*:

> When *Pedal to the Meddle* was first displayed, an upturned seven-metre-long dugout canoe was strapped onto the roof of

the car. The canoe, part of the museum's permanent collection, is decorated with the distinctive red and black Haida stylized forms: the front for example depicts a dogfish. It was designed and carved in 1984 by Bill Reid with the assistance of the Haida carver, Guujaaw and the Kwakwaka'wakw carvers, Simon and Beau Dick. (99)

I single this piece out in particular for several reasons. First, *Pedal to the Meddle* suggests the survivance of Haida culture into the present day by presenting a contemporary mode of transport with one that has been used for centuries, both of which were decorated by Haida artists. Second, this work combines a piece from a permanent museum collection with a comparatively inexpensive hatchback not known for its aesthetics nor prized by car collectors, demonstrating Yahgulanaas's interest in blurring the lines between "high art" and "low art," which is akin to the blurring of the lines drawn between "traditional" and "modern" or even "art" and "material culture." Perhaps most importantly, *Pedal to the Meddle* was intended to be interactive, but the "mounting system precluded the possibility of visitors opening the car doors and sitting inside." Although not realized, this impulse "reflects Yahgulanaas's anti-Kantian notion of his artworks as interactive hybrid objects that can foster intercultural dialogue" (Levell 2016, 99). Yahgulanaas's work generally—as we will see in his graphic novels—is specifically designed to encourage dialog based on active audience participation as opposed to passive (even if reverential, as one might be at a museum) consumption.

In a similar vein, Yahgulanaas is also a popular speaker on issues related to social justice and community building.[6] Although recently "the primary focus of Yahgulanaas's artistic output was the unhalting capitalistic spoliation of Haida Gwaii's natural habitats" (Levell 2016, 21), Yahgulanaas has long been engaged in producing art addressing pressing social issues, particularly those important to Indigenous populations continuing to live with the pressures of settler colonialism. One of the many possible approaches to a work like *Pedal to the Meddle* involves noting the change in spelling of the last word (altered from the common automotive phrase "pedal to the metal" to note racing at high speeds) to suggest that the car is a piece of material culture from the "meddling" settler-colonists and their insistence on technological advancement (even as it damages the natural environment). And while Yahgulanaas's designs on the car can be praised for their aesthetic beauty, the viewer is simultaneously invited to compare the environmentally bad, factory-produced (and thus likely economically exploitative), and now fashionably out-of-date vehicle unfavorably against the environmentally sound, hand-carved, sleek canoe. However, the Haida designs on both vehicles simultaneously suggest that the Haida community persists despite the technologically driven, environmentally destructive developments of settler colonialism. And perhaps more importantly in terms of his artistic development, Yahgulanaas, and Haida artists like him, will find ways to embrace new materials and forms in order to develop Haida art. In his own words:

> I like to adhere to one of the basic Haida tenets or traditions if you must, the tradition of innovation. All material culture, and I suppose intellectual culture is constantly adapting to changes of circumstance. Culture is alive, responsive, engaged and changing. Because I reject the idea of a singular cultural dominance or exclusivity, my work creates places for people to discover an emotional connection with other people, even when they feel those people are strange, distant and even alien. (qtd. in Levell 2016, 47)

For Yahgulanaas, grounding his work in his culture does not preclude working with new forms, new materials, and new influences; similarly, it does not mean repeating traditional designs, images, and narratives in contemporary media. Rather, continual reinvention—through a commitment to innovation, or what I am here calling "experimentation"—is itself a central tenet of Haida cultural expression. And while we can certainly see this in his sculpture and installation art, I would like to now turn to Yahgulanaas's graphic novels to chart the development of what has come to be called "Haida manga."

In addition to being related to the Edenshaws, Yahgulanaas also studied Chinese brush techniques under noted Cantonese master Cai Ben Kwon (Michael Nicoll Yahgulanaas, n.d.-a.), demonstrating his interest in cultivating techniques from a variety of sources, each of which carries on an ancient cultural tradition. Such study prepared him to create the hybrid visual art form he now calls "Haida manga," which is an example of traditional Haida visual art composed by Chinese brush strokes in order to create a graphic narrative that employs characters and colorings drawn from the Japanese manga tradition of graphic narrative. Art critic and curator Ian M. Thom (2009) characterizes Haida manga as "vivid yellows, reds and blues against a white background . . . with a vibrancy and life which suggest the transparency of watercolour and an acute sensitivity to the power of light itself" (174). However, as Thom also notes, Yahgulanaas did not start calling his work "Haida manga" until his "Japanese students . . . compared his work to manga and assured him that it was a respectable art form in their homeland" (171).[7] This is important to note because, as we will see below in the discussion of *Red*, Yahgulanaas is particularly interested in his audience's active participation in the creation of the art and its meaning, here allowing his audience to define his work, and the resulting definition then inspired him to continue further down that particular aesthetic path. The way by which he invites his readers into the process of both art and meaning making is but one of the means by which, in Thom's words, Yahgulanaas "sees that [the larger traditions of Haida art] must evolve and tell new stories, or interpret the old stories in new ways" (175). And by reading multiple graphic novels by Yahgulanaas, we can chart one example of such an evolution.[8]

A Tale of Two Shamans[9] provides a single narrative for what Yahgulanaas (2001) describes, in an introductory note, as "accounts recorded at the turn of the century in three of the once numerous dialects of the Haida language," which constitutes "a contemporary rendering of a worldview first expressed in different times and probably for different reasons." Here, Yahgulanaas notes the traditional nature of the narrative—which would be as familiar to many of his Haida readers as it would be unfamiliar to many readers outside of the Haida community—as well as the fragmentary nature of the source material that he is drawing from (with a subtle but powerful reminder that the dialects—and the stories carried by those dialects—have been disappearing). However, he does not posit his narrative as in any way authoritative, specifically informing the readers to "be cautioned that these images are interpretations informed by my own cultural composition and life experience. . . . I am not stepping forward to join the dais filled with authorities claiming to represent those distant times." In fact, he notes that the historical nature of the texts—documenting life experiences he does not share—puts him in the position of his audience: this "makes us both readers." By not positioning himself as the authority, Yahgulanaas is inviting his readers to engage in the process of meaning making with him as members of a larger interpretive community that he wants to participate in rather than dominate, demonstrating his commitment to creating "places for people to discover an emotional connection with other people" noted above. This also explains his decision to "limiting my retelling to a brief text and illustrations" as opposed to "writing an extensive opinion" (n.p. v). The bulk of the narrative recounting the adventures of Elder, Big Shaman, and their encounter with Spirit Dangerous to Offend, in other words, will be carried by the visual art in full-page renderings on the right with very brief snippets of text on the left-facing page (with the exception of the four two-page visuals and the opening page, none of which have accompanying text).

Readers familiar with wordless novels and works drawn from that tradition should have no problem reading the opening of this narrative, with the first page setting the scene in an idyllic natural landscape and the following establishing the close relationship between Elder and Big Shaman. Later pages depict fishing, hunting, and other events, including their encounters with Spirit Dangerous to Offend. However, the accompanying text helps readers (such as myself) who are unfamiliar with the story and the characters; that is to say, readers unfamiliar with versions of this story may not find the visual narrative to be fully explanatory, especially as some of the pages do not employ the paneling—clearly demarcated frames and gutters—that many readers of graphic narratives rely on to delineate individual scenes and the progression of action. Writing of Yahgulanaas's (2009) use of the formline to replace the gutter in *Red* (though it applies to all of Yahgulanaas's work), Richard Harrison (2016) characterizes the gutter as "a substantial darkness, a sinewy, winding torque that cannot be interpreted or mistaken for a black-or-white vacancy," claiming that "this gutter is meant to have shape and mass, the exact opposite of the convention. This gutter's influence does not stop at the panel borders" (54). The work more commonly done by frames and the gutter is, in Yahgulanaas's work, done by his repurposing of the Haida formline, the dark, heavy line that dominates much of Haida (and other northwestern Indigenous communities) visual art, and which can be employed as the central design element itself to create shapes and figures or as a border separating other design elements; and, like the gutter in mainstream comic art, it can serve both functions simultaneously, as we will see in Yahgulanaas's art.

For instance, in figure 4.2, we see the formline being used to articulate four separate panels underneath a stylized Haida eye, an image common among Haida formline art. The four "panels" at the bottom of the page depict Elder skinning an otter (top left), Elder presenting that otter skin to Big Shaman (top right), Elder failing to properly prepare the otter's hide (bottom left), and a close-up of Big Shaman watching (bottom right). The accompanying text characterizes these images as follows: "That night, in the house, Elder began to skin the otter. The shaman noticed that Elder was unable to properly prepare the otter's hide. 'Give me the skin.'" (Yahgulanaas 2001, 18). The close-up on Big Shaman's eye, then, signals to the reader his intense focus on Elder's failed attempt while serving as a visual parallel to the stylized eye at the top left of the page, perhaps suggesting to the reader that the watching is as important to the narrative as the preparation of the hide. In this example, the formline—curving as it does around the four individual panels—serves to articulate those panels, albeit in a way that simultaneously employs a common Haida design element; the formline, in other words, provides a Haida aesthetic to a page depicting the actions of a traditional Haida narrative, so that the visual presentation as well as the story itself are both examples of traditional Haida art (as opposed to a page with four clearly articulated boxes with a gutter between them found throughout much mainstream comic art). However, Yahgulanaas gives the formline much more interpretive meaning in figure 4.3, where we can identify four separately articulated panels: a lodge and totem pole establishing the scene (top left), Big Shaman's body being pulled out of his coffin (top right), a close-up on an eye shedding a tear (bottom left), and Big Shaman's skin being flayed (bottom right). These images are explained in the accompanying text as follows: "The two paddlers pulled the

Figure 4.2. Michael Nicoll Yahgulanaas, *A Tale of Two Shamans*.

corpse out of the coffin. They wiggled the dead shaman's head, and pulled off the skin" (38).

While the formline does serve to separate these four panels, allowing them to be read as a series of events that contribute to the larger narrative, we can also see how the formline is employed as an important part of action in some of these panels as well. Most strikingly, perhaps, is the dark bump upon which the bird sits in what we could

Figure 4.3. Michael Nicoll Yahgulanaas, *A Tale of Two Shamans*.

call "panel 2," which also serves as the hat worn by the character who pulls the corpse out of the coffin and flays its skin, properly identifying him for the reader. Similarly, what looks like an underscored line to more clearly delineate "panels" 1 and 3 can also be read as an eyebrow, providing more detail to the teary eye. And the formline that separates "panels" 3 and 4 is also the arm of the character removing the skin from Big Shaman, erasing any distinction between "frame" and "character within the frame." The formline itself is also heavily stylized even when not performing such double duty, such as we see with the central vertical line, which is curved and also contains white shapes within it (in this case, an oval and a thin shape with three points, one at the top and two at the bottom). Similarly, at the far left of the central horizontal line we see a foot, which could suggest that much of the formline should be read as the body of the character flaying Big Shaman's skin, perhaps suggesting his importance to these events, making him quite literally the "central" character.

With his use of the formline, then, Yahgulanaas replicates the kind of panel articulation characteristic of mainstream comic art, stylizing the "frames" and "gutter" in such a way as to make them thoroughly Haida. As such, the formal characteristics of the graphic narrative—the formal comic-book elements as well as the narrative itself—represent Haida artistic traditions. In other words, this is a "Haida comic" and not just a Haida story told in comic-book form. The emphasis on Haida culture is also evident from the paratextual inclusion, at the end of the narrative, of what he terms an "interlinear translation" (Yahgulanaas 2001, 85) of the source material: the Haida source text in italics, underneath of which is a literal translation of the words, phrases, and grammatical units, underneath which is a translation in grammatically correct English. *A Tale of Two Shamans* can be read, then, as an innovative use of Haida artistic design to tell a traditional Haida story in a manner reminiscent of—and readable to contemporary readers generally familiar with—comic-book artistry. Its central mode of experimentation is in the use of the formline as a way to stylize common comic-book art elements in a way that pays homage to traditional Haida aesthetics, thus making the work a contemporary example of traditional art and engaging in "the tradition of innovation," which Yahgulanaas noted above is at the center of a Haida aesthetic. And I should also note that Yahgulanaas is not yet using the phrase "Haida manga" to characterize this development, even though he employs the Chinese brush techniques in creating this work.[10] However, in his evolution as an artist, he embraces the connection his students made between his art and Japanese manga with his next work, which more explicitly employs visual techniques drawn from manga artists while simultaneously continuing to work with Haida design elements in the telling of a traditional Haida story.

With the 2009 publication of *Red*, his most famous graphic novel
to date, Yahgulanaas fully embraced the idea of "Haida manga," using
that phrase in the book's subtitle. Additionally, whereas *A Tale of Two
Shamans* was published in black and white, *Red* employs the vibrant
colors of Japanese manga, with primary colors dominating much of
the individual pages. Similarly, akin to manga (and in keeping with his
earlier work as well), Yahgulanaas draws exaggerated facial features on
his characters to better express emotion, particularly in those scenes
where there is little to no accompanying text. And like many other
examples of experimental work, efforts have been made to normalize *Red* by comparing it to works that might be more familiar to the
reading audience. In addition to the overt connections to manga,
which has become increasingly popular in North America, the inside
jacket cover, for instance, notes that it is "reminiscent of such classic
stories as *Oedipus Rex* and *Macbeth*," two texts perennially popular
among high-school and college instructors in the English-speaking
world. And while there is much productive analysis that can come
from such a cross-cultural analysis, doing so could (unintentionally)
lead a reader to ignore what makes this work distinctive and thus lose
sight of the important cultural work done by Yahgulanaas. Rather, I
would prefer to read *Red* in a continuum with his earlier and later
graphic novels, to highlight both the experimental nature of his works
as well as their importance as a manifestation of Haida survivance.

Referencing not only how *Red* is often characterized by readers
but also (albeit unintentionally) how much Indigenous experimental
narrative is characterized by scholars, Miriam Brown Spiers (2014)
writes that "*Red* is not simply a mash-up of popular genres; rather, it
is the work of a traditionally trained Haida artist who is respectful
of the culture and artistic traditions out of which he has emerged."
Perhaps more importantly, however, Spiers also notes, "Even though
Yahgulanaas's adaptation of Haida art is vastly different from the work
that has come before it, the Haida manga actually maintains and reinforces both the rules of the traditional art and the beliefs of the Haida
people" (52). These are important points. First, this is not simply Haida
art with manga flourishes, or what Richard Harrison (2016) characterizes as "traditional Haida visual representations . . . with the dynamics
of manga" (52); rather, it is an interpretation of traditional Haida art

engaging new compositional and narrative elements.[11] Second, and just as importantly, the manga elements work in concert with the overall Haida aesthetic to enhance the Haida cultural elements, which Spiers (2014) defines as "the importance of balance in both art and life" (41). Telling the story of Red, a prideful Haida leader who sought to enact vengeance on those who, years ago, abducted his sister, Red is a warning about the destructive nature of revenge, an impulse that brings people out of balance with themselves and their communities. Yahgulanaas uses all the formal devices at his disposal—including the formline—to convey this message to his audience.

Given the importance of the formline throughout his narrative art, any analysis of Red should begin with an understanding of his use of it in place of the gutter (and clearly articulated panels), the significance of which has been central to the few scholars who have published on Red. In addition to Harrison's comments quoted above, Spiers focuses on the formline as the central characteristic for her reading of social responsibility in Red. Spiers (2014) reminds her readers that, whereas (sometimes) the gutter is a secondary space created as the result of panels, in Yahgulanaas's work, the "gutter" is an active space and, at times, the primary space for aesthetic craft and meaning making: "In many comics, the artist can build the frame as a way of containing the narrative, but in the case of Red, Yahgulanaas has to find a way to tell the story across *a space that had already been claimed by the formline*" (42; emphasis added). As I will discuss in more detail below, the formline was created first, and the remaining visual elements had to be placed around it in order to tell the story. The formline as a material part of the story (as opposed to merely a space separating panels) is noted on the first page of the text, where one of the characters grips the top piece of the formline to steady himself as he looks at the rushing water depicted below. Two pages later, Red (the title character) is saved from drowning by his sister, who holds onto the formline for support as she pulls him out of the ocean.[12] Similar examples (as well as many others) can be found throughout the book, demonstrating how the formline separates the various "panels" while simultaneously acting as an operative, material component in those same panels, such as in figure 4.4, where again the formline is held onto as part of the ship carrying passengers.

Figure 4.4. Michael Nicoll Yagulanaas, *Red: A Haida Manga*.

And like its use in *A Tale of Two Shamans*, the formline as a panel separator in *Red* creates some very unconventional panels, such as we see in figure 4.5.

Here, the page is broken up into five irregularly shaped panels (and one small piece of negative space on the upper left of the page), all created from the curved lines common in Haida design. However, as Spiers (2014) notes, this has no effect on the narrative itself, and the "anatomical relationship" between the panels, "their chronological order, is still basically retained" (42–43). Rather than impede the readers' understanding of the narrative, Spiers argues that the use of the formline provides additional meaning, given that "in a world

Figure 4.5. Michael Nicoll Yagulanaas, *Red: A Haida Manga*.

where the boundaries are so flexible, it becomes imperative that each person is aware of her connections and the power of her actions." Because "boundaries are not hard and fast formal characteristics but actually organic elements, then any boundary can be disrupted by any character or, really, any other part of the world" (46). Recounting Red's attempts to rescue his sister years after she had been captured—which ultimately leads to his untimely and unnecessary death because of his headstrong actions—the formline emphasizes the story's call for flexibility and adaptation.[13]

As a now characteristic part of Yahgulanaas's graphic storytelling, the formline is a richly developed component of both the aesthetic and narrative aspects of the work. However, its primary importance in *Red* is what truly makes this work "experimental." As noted above, the other features of the work had to be developed secondarily to the formline; the formline was crafted first, with the story then "filling in" the spaces between the formline. Such an approach—essentially creating the gutter first, then crafting the narrative around the gutter—is an unconventional approach to comic-book art and sequential storytelling. Perhaps just as importantly, for Katherine Kelp-Stebbins (2020), this unconventional panel layout also "challenges the logic of settler-colonialism," particularly in the way it "exposes spatial navigation as a learned process" (89). As such, we can read his attention to the formline as an increasingly political development as well as an aesthetic one. Further, unlike his use of the formline in *A Tale of Two Shamans*—as a stylized replacement for the gutter that emphasized Haida aesthetic principles—the formline in *Red* creates a larger picture, a piece of Haidi visual art that is not evident from the original reading experience.[14]

In a paratextual note following the narrative, Yahgulanaas (2009) invites his readers to "destroy this book," to "rip the pages out of their bindings" so that the pages can be arranged as a larger piece of Haida visual art, one that is intended to "defy your ability to experience story as a simple progression of events" (n.p.). In one respect, then, the pages of the book can be arranged to present the narrative on one "page," not unlike what some artists have done with large paintings and murals.[15] Spiers (2014) notes the narrative importance of this possibility: "That the book is also a mural is another way of reminding readers of . . . interconnectedness: because we can step outside of a single panel or even a single page and view the story as a unified whole, we can understand that each action in each frame has the ability to affect the bigger picture in a very literal sense" (47). The compositional elements of the (potential) mural—like the compositional elements of the sequential narrative—thus beautifully emphasize the narrative's central theme.

However, Yahgulanaas is also encouraging his readers to see *Red* as more than just a book and to see themselves as more than just his audience. *Red* is also a collection of materials that the reader can use to create something new, something not at all visible when reading it as a bound narrative.[16] The book is both a book as well as a starter kit for the reader's attempt to help create a large-scale piece of Haida art. In *A Tale of Two Shamans*, Yahgulanaas envisioned himself as a "reader" in the company of those reading his book; with *Red*, he invites the readers to join him as cocreators of the work of art, as the kind of active participants he envisioned for his installation piece *Pedal to the Meddle*. Writing of Yahgulanaas's sparse use of words that forces the readers to "take an active role in the storytelling," Spiers (2014) notes that this kind of "participatory reading practice is similar to Native oral storytelling traditions, which also demand a level of audience/reader involvement that may be difficult to reproduce in text-based novels" (50–51). Although not itself part of the reading practice, the reader's participation in the creation of the mural—an action that must be completed by the reader after being provided the raw materials by Yahgulanaas—brings her into another level of audience participation, perhaps even frustrating the boundary between artist and audience that emphasizes Yahgulanaas's belief, noted above, that "culture is alive, responsive, engaged and changing."[17] The reader thus not only engages with a "Haida manga" but also participates in the construction of a new piece of cocreated Haida art. The full aesthetic and cultural impact, therefore, cannot be achieved through the act of reading alone and requires the cooperation of the reader to continue the work that Yahgulanaas began.

Described on the cover as a "Haida manga" and thus demonstrating Yahgulanaas's continuing identification with that cross-cultural hybrid aesthetic, *War of the Blink* presents another ancient Haida narrative, one that "took place long before there was a Canada or a United States," as Yahgulanaas (2017) offers in a prefatory note. Such a statement historicizes the story for the reader but also highlights Yahgulanaas's persistent use of his work to engage in Haida survivance, particularly when he reminds his readers that "it should not be a surprise that there are peoples who remember when there was no such thing as a Canada or a United States." As with his earlier work, which subtly invited readers outside the Haida community to participate in the artistic creation, here, Yahgulanaas directly confronts the audience with the reminder that he and his people cultivate memories that "are not discarded but remain alive and are actively refreshed" (n.p. i). However, in contrast to the two rather serious stories presented in his earlier books, *War of the Blink* is a humorous rendition of a staring contest between the leaders of two neighboring nations that prevented an actual war. For while the champions from each nation were staring one another down while fighting, a fly (introduced earlier in the text but whose purpose was not revealed until later) passed between them, causing one of the warriors to blink. That blink ended the hostilities, and the combatants—and eventually the two nations—became friends. And because the point of the book is to celebrate the friendship—to celebrate the continuation of positive community building—"it really doesn't matter who blinked first" (n.p. 54). The narrative ends with the note that "even up to this very day these peoples still have dinners together" (n.p. 55), highlighting the importance of the sustained peace that can come from two previously hostile communities.

Although all three of his books highlight the importance of community building—even if the first two were presented more as cautionary tales—*War of the Blink* employs a degree of humor not found in *A Tale of Two Shamans* and *Red*. That said, Yahgulanaas continues to develop the visual aesthetic of "Haida manga" in several ways. First, like *Red*, *War of the Blink* employs characters with overemphasized visual features, against a backdrop of beautifully rendered scenery, all of which is depicted with the use of bright colors. But more importantly, Yahgulanaas once again employs a complexly rendered formline that both separates and becomes part of the panels. For instance, at various points the formline is used as a body part or the side of a canoe, where sometimes characters will rest a hand or drape an arm alongside. However, the formline is also put to a new use.

In figure 4.6, the formline separates the top scene of Gunee paddling from the bottom scene where he is fishing. But the formline is also the current of water that Gunee paddles in, in a scene that can be read as a different view of the top "panel" (the position of the hands and direction of the head are the same) as well as a separate scene (a third panel) given that the formline does not constitute the water through which Gunee paddles in the top scene. Often colored dark blue instead of black, the formline is used as a waterway multiple times elsewhere in the book. With *War of the Blink*, then, Yahgulanaas continues to find new ways to employ the formline in his work, new

Figure 4.6. Michael Nicoll Yahgulanaas, *War of the Blink*.

uses for an ancient aesthetic to tell ancient stories that appeal to the visual interests of a contemporary comic-book readership.

And just as the various pages of *Red* can be removed and assembled into a mural that also recounts the narrative, so too do the pages of *War of the Blink* create a larger work of visual art for the reader (figure 4.7).

However, there are two noticeable differences. First, the author does not encourage his readers to remove the pages and construct

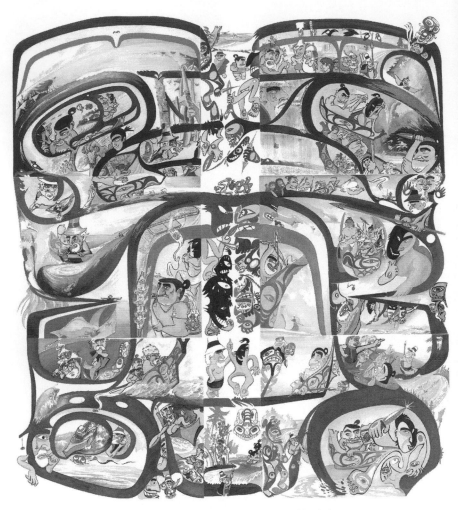

Figure 4.7. Michael Nicoll Yahgulanaas, *War of the Blink*.

the narrative. Perhaps this is because, having done so once already, he trusts his readers to be able to do so on their own, should they so desire. Secondly, and perhaps more importantly, in order to create their own copy of the mural,[18] readers will have to assemble the pages out of their narrative order. Having already created one formline image for *Red*, it's possible that Yahgulanaas wanted to avoid duplicating the same design; a new story may require a new formline (and, as such, a new sequential logic). The individual pages could constitute puzzle pieces that the reader can use to assemble the larger picture, shown at the end of the book. As such, the formline thus becomes the guiding visual principle to assemble this puzzle. However, the invitation to do so is not made explicit as it was in *Red*. Perhaps Yahgulanaas is merely sharing the original painting with his audience, with no suggestion (explicit or otherwise) to craft something new out of the pages of his book. Speaking of *Red*, Yahgulanaas notes:

> Individual templates . . . are jigsawed together with others to create a singular large mural. The theme for that interactivity is the core story idea behind *Red* which is "what do we do when all we believe to be true turns out to be false?" I hope to encourage individuals to see that such situations are not at all unique and these shared and frequently unsettling experiences can become the basis for increasing collective identity. (qtd. in Levell 2016, 91)

In contrast to *Red*, *War of the Blink* does not present a story that asks readers to rethink what they might know to be true (as Red learns that the vengeful ways he believes to be helpful are in fact harmful), nor does it present a community that has been fragmented by a kidnapping or a needless death. So, just as there is no fragmentation within the community, there is no invitation to engage with the text as a collection of fragments in need of a larger whole. But ultimately, the point is that Yahgulanaas is not simply repeating an old trick in a new volume. While the visual aesthetic of "Haida manga" has certainly developed over the three books, each work should certainly be read—and otherwise engaged with—on its own terms and not just as a replication of what came before. As quoted above, Yahgulanaas is committed to the idea that "culture is alive, responsive, engaged and changing."

• • •

Whereas Yahgulanaas uses his formal experimentations to present Haida art and cultural traditions to a wide readership, eelonqa K. harris[19] employs a type of formal experimentation that highlights the people who serve as the basis for the characters in her recent books *Nighthawk and Little Elk* (2017) and *Blueberry Boy* (2018).[20] Harris (e.g., 2017) herself highlights the central importance of this experimentation by noting at the end of each book: "If there is only one thing you know about this book, it should be that the characters are only 12 inches tall. They are "avatars," hand-crafted by the author/illustrator, created with the aid of a 3D printer, action figure bodies, alpaca hair, miniature clothing, custom fabrics, tiny accessories, enormous amounts of time, extensive resources, and a whole lot of creativity" (30). Rather than drawing the panels, as is common in most graphic novels, each panel is a staged photograph, most of which feature some of the avatars (some photographs are purely scenery), some of which have been digitally altered (overlaying images on top of one another, altering the colors, etc.). This process is akin to that famously used by Alison Bechdel to create her award-winning graphic memoir *Fun Home*. For *Fun Home*—in a departure from the more straightforward composition process she used in her series *Dykes to Watch Out For*—Bechdel (2006) drew the panels largely from photographs that she staged herself and for which she posed as every character (in addition to using existing photographs). This painstaking process is one reason why Bechdel spent seven years in crafting *Fun Home*, and harris similarly notes above the "enormous amounts of time" she spent on her work. Such a process is also similar to that used by Elbe Spurling for her book series *The Brick Bible*, which illustrates the Bible with the use of staged LEGO characters and settings.[21] In all three cases, the artist is staging photographs, with Bechdel taking an additional step of drawing panels based on those photographs, whereas Spurling and harris use the photographs directly.

Like Spurling, harris is using avatars in her work, albeit those based off of real people instead of an iconic toy.[22] And like Bechdel, harris is representing real people, even if many of Bechdel's drawing of her family are based on photographs of herself. Whereas one can read a degree of realism in Bechdel's work, that realism is at least two steps removed (a drawn character based on a photograph of the author). With harris's work, the sense of realism is more present, given that the avatars were created to look like specific people playing roles in the narrative. In fact, at the end of each book, harris includes a cast list, with photographs of the real people next to the avatars they posed for (figure 4.8).[23] And by presenting this as a "cast," harris is aligning this work to live-action acting, such as we would see on stage or on the screen. The focus here is on the real people, who we should see as artistic cocreators and not merely as physical models for the characters.

And here is where we see the cultural importance of her experimentation. Whereas Indigenous creators have been woefully underrepresented in both academic studies and in bookstore shelf space, Indigenous peoples themselves have been poorly represented in much (non-Indigenous) comics and graphic novels (not to mention on stage and screen). As is the case with much literature, film, and advertising that makes use of Indigenous characters, those characters are often drawn from popular stereotypes.[24] With her two recent books, harris thus seeks to challenge that lack of representation by casting actual Indigenous people into the roles of her narratives and physically constructing 3D-printed avatars modeled on those individuals, marking a turn similar to that taken by Hollywood when directors started to cast actual Indigenous people in Indigenous roles.[25] In addition to serving the goal of diversifying the fields of comics and graphic novels by including more Indigenous peoples in the various stages of creation for her works, the use of actual Indigenous people additionally confronts stereotyping by giving representations of real people, not all of whom will share identical traits that may mark them for the audience as "Indians" (think, for instance, of the large nose that became a notable feature in "spaghetti westerns"); a quick scan of the cast for both books reveals individuals with different facial features and skin tones, all of whom were cast (presumably) for how well they best fit the needed role(s) (with some people being used as inspiration for multiple avatars in a single book).

Further, in *Blueberry Boy* harris also uses photographs of various objects throughout the narrative as additional visual information situated outside of the panels. While in some cases these are common items, such as bottles of milk and Coca-Cola (harris 2018, 8), the more striking examples are the "Wolfman and pipe carving" (3) and the "sturgeon carving" (22) we see in figure 4.9, both created by Shannon Peters, who was the model for Blueberry Boy's grandmother. These images themselves are photorealistic even while the background

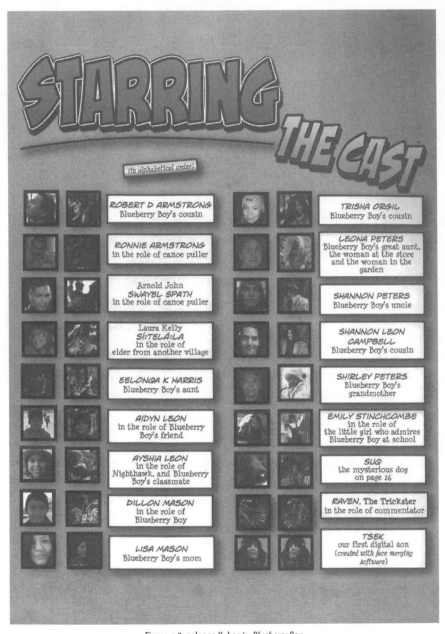

Figure 4.8. eelonqa K. harris, *Blueberry Boy*.

Figure 4.9. eelonqa K. harris, *Blueberry Boy*.

on the page is not; this dichotomy both highlights the realism of the artifacts while also reminding the reader of the mediated nature of this narrative, one that is based on real people and their works but in a heavily stylized manner.

In addition to the 3D-printed avatars representing actual Indigenous individuals, harris also includes photographs of the artwork created by one of those individuals (whom she credits in a textbox on the bottom of the page), highlighting the artistic creations of her community members. In doing so, harris subtly suggests that these various community members are people with various skills and talents that also deserve recognition, another means of artistic cocreation. With her focus on the visual representation of actual Indigenous people and their artistic creations, harris is using her graphic novel to promote representation of Indigenous arts as well as Indigenous peoples, providing a rich layer of additional meaning to the narratives themselves. Harris's interest in connecting her readers to real-world people and events is further emphasized in *Nighthawk and Little Elk* when she invites her readers to "google" "The Sixties Scoop," which forms the basis of "the deeper underlying topic of this story" (2017, 30),[26] and in *Blueberry Boy* when she notes that the book "is designed to educate, entertain, inspire, share experiences, and foster communication" (2018, 29). In a very different manner, she shares with fellow experimental graphic novelist Michael Nicoll Yahgulanaas a desire to involve her audience directly in extratextual engagement while also employing a kind of formal experimentation that emphasizes the art of their communities.

As such, we see an Indigenous artist on the forefront of employing a relatively new technology—3D printing—in the service of creating comic-book art, opening up new directions for future comic-book artists. And it should be noted that, despite this new method of "casting" characters for graphic novels, the rest of the artwork falls squarely within what readers familiar with comic-book art might expect.

As we see in figure 4.10, for instance, the avatars are situated within a clearly identified panel, framed above and below with printed narrative text. Harris also uses the familiar speech bubbles for character speech and includes aural cues to note the sound made by the fire. The formal experimentation with respect to character representation,

Figure 4.10. eelonqa K. harris, *Nighthawk and Little Elk*.

then, is situated within the more familiar formal properties of comic-book art and, as such, highlights the experimental nature of the use of avatars. In other words, the experimentation stands out even more by contrast, highlighting for the reader the importance of the use of real, Indigenous peoples in her work. So, as much as *Nighthawk and Little Elk* is a retelling of (in harris's [2017] words) a "local aboriginal take of an infamous witch" woven together with "the author's own fiction" and the Brothers Grimm story "Brüderchen und Schwesterchen" (30), the focus can rightly be placed on the importance of the representation of the actual Indigenous people who are reimaged as characters in the narrative. This may be even more so the case for *Blueberry Boy*, given that "Blueberry Boy is the author's nephew" (harris 2018, 29).

• • •

Both Michael Nicoll Yahgulanaas and eelonqa K. harris engage in kinds of formal experimentation that not only offer comic-book artists new possibilities for their own creations but also draw attention to the Indigenous communities they belong to. Through his use of the formline to replace and give additional meaning to the gutter, Yahgulanaas highlights the endlessly malleable possibilities open to artists for framing the panels and, more importantly, for representing the visual flow of the narrative on (and off, in the case of the murals) the page. In her use of avatars modeled off of actual community members, harris explores a new means of visualizing and representing characters on the page. More importantly, both of these forms of experimentation also engage the racial politics of these books in the ways that they engage in and actively promote Indigenous communities and their arts. Remembering Beth Berila's (2005) claim that "multiethnic experimental literature often reveals how meaning production is deeply embedded in the shifting categories of race, ethnicity, gender, sexuality, and nation" (32), we can recognize how Yahgulanaas's use of the formline highlights a cultural fluidity between traditional Haida art and Japanese manga, allowing the reader to see the cross-cultural similarities between two communities most likely seen as distinct, as well as how harris's use of avatars crafted to look like members of her tribal community highlights the lack of accurate Indigenous representation on the page. In both cases, the formal experimentation is not simply experimentation for the sake of experimentation; the experimentation is drawn from and ultimately refers the audience back to the rich cultures from which these artists draw their inspiration. For the audience outside of those communities, such work invites the readers to learn more about the art, culture, and history of the author's Indigenous communities. But for those readers who belong to those communities, these works offer a unique opportunity to see their art and culture highlighted in ways that do not otherwise exist in the increasingly popular comic-book arts.

In a completely different vein, while this was certainly not a consideration when writing this chapter, both Michael Nicoll Yahgulanaas and eelonqa K. harris belong to northwest coastal First Nations communities. Although I would not recommend making any larger aesthetic or political point regarding this coincidence, I would like to highlight it as an important reminder about how and why we discuss Indigenous artists. Throughout this chapter, I noted the importance of community to these two artists and highlighted the ways that these creators used their works to focus attention on, support, or otherwise engage their communities, not to mention the subtle invitations to their readers to become more knowledgeable about those communities. Geographically as well as aesthetically and politically, Yahgulanaas and harris belong to (broadly speaking) the same larger community. I would encourage my readers to consider the variety of ways that the authors discussed in this and the preceding chapters belong to various communities. Although this book paired the authors based on genre, there are a great many ways these authors can be grouped together, some of which will be addressed in the coda.

BUT WAIT, ISN'T THERE MORE?

Oh yes, so much more. By necessity, this book only scratches the surface. Further, not only are there many more books and series than could be included in one academic monograph, but in the time it takes for this book to be reviewed, revised, printed, and placed on library shelves, many more wonderful Indigenous comics and graphic novels will be produced. No one volume could hope to adequately cover the entire field, and so I made no effort to do so. Rather, I focused largely on my own personal interests—the books, series, and authors I most enjoy reading and teaching—as well as where I found some of the most compelling political work being done by Indigenous comic-book artists (admittedly, there is a great deal of overlap in those two categories). Further, not all works will fit quite so neatly into chapters broken down by genre. As we saw in chapter 1, for instance, Stephen Graham Jones's *My Hero* could just as easily have been included in the chapter on experimental narratives as in the chapter on superhero comics. And many superhero stories—such as those penned by Arigon Starr as well as Jones—could be discussed in terms of Indigenous futurism as explored in chapter 2. At the end of the day—or at the end of the book—we must accept that the choices made are nothing more than a starting point in the larger conversation, keeping alive hopes that this book will contribute something useful to the growing field of Indigenous comics studies. And in that vein, I am eager to see others extend, challenge, correct, and fill in the gaps revealed by my own work. There is more; there will always be more. For as long as Indigenous artists are producing such work, no academic study about them can hope to conclude the discussion. The best any of us can do is to point out some exciting paths that others can wander down at their leisure in the hopes that more good work will come from such explorations.

There are also a great many ways that we could classify, organize, and analyze the myriad works being produced throughout the United States and Canada by Indigenous comic-book artists. The organization chosen for this book is simply one way of providing some order to the beautifully chaotic scene of Indigenous comics. Genre, as discussed in the introduction, gives us both a handy means of classifying complex literary works (even if it does so at the risk of oversimplification) as well as a framework for interpretation: genre, in other words, helps readers to understand the work and provides a method for critical engagement. That said, the genres identified in these chapters are not only not exclusive, but they are also not the only possible framework by which readers can come to understand these narratives. That is to say, instead of (or in addition to) the genres chosen above—superhero comics, science fiction comics, historical comics, and experimental comics—chapters could have been devoted to, for instance, war comics. Instead of examining how books like Chag Lowry's *Soldiers Unknown* and Katherena Vermette's ongoing series *A Girl Called Echo* represent the past as a living component of the present, one could just as easily study them for their representations of warfare: How is warfare visually represented? What lessons are to be learned from these conflicts? Such a chapter could also include Arigon Starr's edited collection *Tales of the Mighty Code Talkers*, which collects short graphic stories by many artists discussed in this book.[1] Such a chapter could also include comics depicting fictional wars, noting what we can learn from such events as the futuristic interplanetary war outlined in Todd Houseman's "Ayanisach" from the first volume of *Moonshot* or Daniel H. Wilson's contributions to the DC Earth 2 series *World's End*, which pits familiar DC superheroes, such as Superman and the Flash, against the four furies of Apokolips, one of whom is the manifestation of war itself. Even Michael Nicoll Yahgulanaas's humorous *War of the Blink* could be discussed as a satiric commentary on war, helping readers to understand not only the nature of warfare but also the larger consequences of rhetorically characterizing conflicts as "wars."

Similar cases could be made for a variety of other potential genres, such as adaptations and modernizations of traditional stories, narratives focused on reservation life, or books that have an explicit focus

on preserving and/or teaching Indigenous languages. This last possibility is particularly fascinating given its assumption of the entertainment value of comic-book storytelling (answering the question,
How do we make language preservation and learning "fun"?) and the
various pedagogical possibilities for such books. Cole Pauls's (2017)
Dakwäkãda Warriors, discussed above as an example of Indigenous
futurism rooted in the conventions of science fiction, is also explicitly
a vehicle for the preservation of the "two southern Tutchone dialects—Champagne (Shadhäla Kʼe) and Aishihik (Àshèy Kʼe)" (Pauls
2019, n.p. 115). As he notes in the volume that collects all three comics, Pauls "wanted to make DW a language revival comic so I asked
two language preservers . . . to collaborate" (n.p. 99). All three of the
original comics include numerous words and phrases that the reader
can translate by means of a glossary included at the end of the comics; the 2019 collected volume translates the words and phrases on
the same page, presumably to ease the reader's efforts at learning
these terms (though a "Language Key" also exists at the end of the
volume). That is to say, when these comics were reprinted, there was
a conscious decision to explicitly address the book's use in language
learning, demonstrating a clear pedagogical focus. Kayla Shaggy (2017;
Diné and Annishinabe) employs a similar strategy in her ongoing
series *The Sixth World*, each volume of which includes a "Navajo to
English Glossary" (n.p. 23). Richard Van Camp's (Dogrib Tłıchǫ)
graphic novel *Three Feathers* is also, though in a radically different way,
another example of the use of comic-book storytelling for language
preservation. First published in 2015 as part of the Debwe Series of
Highwater Press, the book was simultaneously published in English
with two additional dual-language editions, one each in Bush Cree
and Chipewyan, with a later (2017) edition published in both English
and Slavey. Each of the dual-language editions can be read entirely
in one language or the other; simply flip the book over to read it in
the alternate language. Unlike *Dakwäkãda Warriors*, which includes
Tutchone words and phrases as part of a largely English-language
narrative, *Three Feathers* provides full narratives in each of the three
Indigenous languages, preserving not just a select terminology but
the cadence of the languages, how they are used in narration and
dialogue, how contemporary speakers might frame discussions. If

the former is meant to help learn the language, the latter assumes a degree of fluency among its readers or at least gives language learners a goal in their continued study of the language.

All that said, other classification systems could be employed to survey the field of Indigenous comics and graphic novels. Some creators—such as David A. Robertson, Michael Nicoll Yahgulanaas, and Jeffrey Veregge (if you include his cover art as well as the stories he has written and published in the *Moonshot* books)—could merit individual chapters that look at their larger body of work (possibly with, but not limited to, biographical studies). Artists from the same tribal nations or language groups could be studied together, particularly with a focus on how those artists use their works to represent cultural histories and traditions.[2] Or, to take a wildly different tack— and remembering Christopher González's (2017) point in *Permissible Narratives: The Promise of Latino/a Literature* that "publishers foisted certain narrative conventions on Latino/a authors" (11) (reminding scholars that publishers often silently but profoundly shape the material that they publish, especially in the case of nonwhite and other politically marginalized authors)—we could productively study comics and graphic novels in the context of their publishers. In the case of such Indigenous-owned and -operated presses, like Native Realities Press, or publishing ventures, like the Debwe Series of Highwater Press, which was founded to exclusively publish Indigenous authors, we are not likely to find the kind of intellectual or artistic bullying that González discusses in his study, though we certainly might in the case of books published by larger presses that do not share a commitment to serving Indigenous communities. But more importantly, such a focus could then allow for a comparison between work published by established presses (such as Native Realities and Highwater) and that published by the authors themselves, as we see with such creators as Theo Tso, who publishes *Captain Paiute* through his War Paint Studio, and Kayla Shaggy, who publishes her books through her Triple Jeopardy Productions.

There are, as I hope I made clear, numerous means by which we could approach a critical study of Indigenous comics and graphic novels, discussing their aesthetic, political, and cultural importance, not to mention the effect they have on diverse groups of readers. Ultimately, however, *how* we study these works is secondary to the very necessity of studying them at all. As witnessed by the various job openings in the field, the myriad college courses that regularly run (in and out of Indigenous studies programs), and the rising number of focused academic monographs, the study of Indigenous literature—especially fiction, creative nonfiction (particularly life writing), and poetry—has become a stable branch on the larger tree of academic literary studies. Similarly, comics studies is increasingly taking on a similar stature in the larger field. That said, Indigenous comics are rarely studied in the larger context of Indigenous literatures, and Indigenous-created works are glaringly absent from most of the discussions taking place in comics studies.[3]

More than a decade ago, Matthew Herman (2010) noted: "From what it demonstrates about the political nature and function of contemporary Native American literature, the question about *how* popular culture is redefining the status of Native American writing also cannot be ignored. As should become readily apparent, popular culture functions as a textual space in which culture and politics converge" (105). And although he was not explicitly writing about comics and graphic novels, his comments are certainly doubly prescient in that regard. Indigenous artists are increasingly turning to comics and graphic novels, with publishers like Native Realities and Highwater Press carving out space for Indigenous creators that major comic-book publishers seem as yet unwilling to provide. Further, despite their growing acceptance in formal academic studies, comics and graphic novels have never ceded their position as popularly consumed culture: sales of comics and graphic novels continue to climb, and the TV/movie industry regularly adapts these narratives into films and TV series. And Indigenous creators also know what non-Indigenous creators have long known to be true: readers will find these works, consume them, and celebrate them.[4]

It is time that the larger field of literary studies devotes the time and attention to these works that their artistry merits.

ACKNOWLEDGMENTS

There is not the proper time, space, or language to allow me to express my gratitude to all who contributed to the research, writing, and publication of this book. On this page, I hope to do justice to just a few of the many people without whom this book could not have been written.

First, I would like to thank all those whose thoughts, insights, and support have assisted me in the various stages of this work. A great many scholars, like Jeremy M. Carnes, unknowingly helped me clarify my thinking through their presentations at conferences or thoughtful questions on my own presentations. As always, professional conferences remain one of the best opportunities for academics to test, revise, and rethink ideas with fellow travelers. Similarly, an even larger number of students in my classes have generously responded to my thoughts about some of these works as we explored them in the classroom, a very different but no less important kind of intellectual proving ground. And numerous professionals like Janine Utell and Gene Kannenberg provided direct assistance by answering a variety of questions I had at the outset of this project. However, I owe the greatest of thanks to my friend and mentor Frederick Luis Aldama, who has been a champion for this project from its inception through its acceptance by the University Press of Mississippi.

I could not have asked for better treatment from an academic press, and I would like to thank all those at the University Press of Mississippi for their hard work on publishing this book. In particular, I owe a debt I cannot repay to Lisa McMurtray and Michael Martella, both of whom are the very model of professionalism and without whose work this book would be nothing more than a series of files on my computer. I am similarly thankful for the careful eye and thoughtful attention of Laura J. Vollmer, whose editing cleaned up many of the errors and other small infelicities peppered throughout the text.

Special thanks must be extended to Pete Halverson for designing the cover. And words cannot express how grateful I am that Michael Nicoll Yahgulanaas gave us permission to use his beautiful art for the cover. I am also grateful to the two external reviewers for this project, whose insights and suggestions undoubtedly improved this work. In particular, I offer my hearty thanks to Susan Bernardin, who highlighted a number of problematic issues found throughout the manuscript. In particular, she provided useful information about one of the authors and corrected some of my earlier attributions. Although often not glamorous work, reviewing books for presses is a critically important part of the process. That said, despite the hard work of these many professionals, any and all errors fall squarely on my shoulders.

I have struggled with how to word this final paragraph, and how best to express my thanks to this final group of people. What follows is correct but hardly expresses all that needs to be said. I started this project before the onset of the global COVID pandemic. And like a great many people, I set such work aside while dealing with the myriad issues we all needed to address. During the subsequent years, we have all had to adjust—and continue to adjust—to the changes in our world. One of the many reasons I returned to this project, and one of the reasons I was able to complete it, was the support from my partner, Kristen Remington, and her three kids, Reid, Jacob, and Fletcher. Their support—whether directly, in encouraging me to finish this work, or indirectly, such as when I snuck glances at them while they themselves were immersed in reading graphic novels—helped sustain me through some of the most difficult stages of this process. But most importantly, they serve as a constant reminder to me to log off from my computer, put down my book, and live my life. They are the very best people I know, and I dedicate this book to them.

NOTES

1. It is probably fitting that the first footnote should attend to terminology, especially given that I have already used both "Indigenous" and "Native American" before finishing the first sentence. Following standard usage in much of the critical literature, I use "Native American" when referring exclusively to US artists and "First Nations, Métis, and Inuit" when referring exclusively to Canadian artists. When referring to the larger group comprised by the two, I use "Indigenous," which is the term most often used in this study. In some cases, the word "Native" is used; this is done to reflect its usage by scholars and artists I am quoting (if this is their preferred terminology) or when referencing previous usage. But most importantly, at all points, tribal affiliation is used when writing about individual artists. My goal here is to be specific when possible. But when referring more generally to the larger group of artists, I want to use terminology that is respectful. I would like to thank an early reviewer of this work for her corrections regarding the proper attribution of tribal affiliation for some of the artists discussed. Any mistakes are certainly my own. Interested readers are directed to Gregory Younging's (2018; Opaskwayak Cree Nation) *Elements of Indigenous Style: A Guide for Writing by and about Indigenous Peoples.*

2. I should note here that Chute is not herself disparaging superhero comics, to which she devotes the second chapter of her book. Rather, she recognizes that, for a great many readers (and, sadly, scholars), such narratives are not taken seriously as literature. Like Chute, I wholeheartedly dismiss such criticism, as will become evident in chapter 1.

3. To be honest, I did consider such an approach in part because, while there are many excellent monographs on Native American and First Nations literatures, as of this writing, none of them include a chapter on comics/graphic novels. I quickly realized, however, that such an approach would only work if I significantly narrowed the focus of the study. A book on Indigenous historical fiction, for example, could include a chapter on comics/graphic novels as well as chapters on fiction, TV and film, music, etc. Ideally, we will begin to see such studies as more scholars with

diverse interests work on Indigenous comics. However, the more time I spent on my research, the more I wanted to focus exclusively on comics.

4. One important exception is Daniel H. Wilson (Cherokee), author of the graphic novel *Quarantine Zone* as well as the creator of multiple issues of the DC Earth 2 sequence. Although many chain bookstores do not carry single-issue comics, the Earth 2 issues were certainly readily available at bookstores that carry the latest DC issues.

5. I would like to note that, in one small example of the press's commitment to Indigenous studies, the press gives its location as follows: "The offices of Portage & Main Press and HighWater Press are located on Treaty 1 Territory as well as the homeland of the Métis Nation" (Portage & Main Press, n.d.). While some may see this as a small gesture, such recognition is one of many steps being taken by organizations committed to increasing recognition and representation, as well as working on behalf of political sovereignty. As we will see below, many of the titles published and distributed by Portage & Main address such issues directly.

6. This event has since spawned similar Indigenous comic-book conventions locally in Denver, Colorado, and internationally in Melbourne, Australia, demonstrating the large and international appeal of events celebrating Indigenous comics specifically and pop culture generally.

7. E-book publications have been a great boon for comics artists but have become an essential publication format for many Indigenous (and other historically marginalized) creators, who are often not carried by national and international distributors.

8. Although the book itself is compellingly written and beautifully illustrated, and thus worthy of study in its own right, it is also the centerpiece of a public exhibition that ran at the Library Company of Philadelphia. Providing materials for various reading events and classroom activities at local universities, this exhibit included Alvitre's original hand-painted artwork, a wampum belt created by Wampanoag artist Elizabeth James-Perry, various historical documents from the period, and a documentary film about the production of the book. In addition to its obvious educational value, this exhibit also brings to much larger popular and academic attention the work of multiple Indigenous artists.

9. Perhaps this is the best time for me to note that I am not myself Indigenous, nor do I have any formal affiliation with any tribal nation. I read, teach, and produce research on Indigenous fiction and comics and teach courses in Native American literature for the State University of New York (SUNY) at Potsdam, a small public university in Haudenosaunee territory, near the Mohawk Nation at Akwesasne.

10. One important article is Susan Bernardin's (2015) "Future Pasts: Comics, Graphic Novels, and Digital Media," included in *The Routledge Companion to Native American Literature* edited by Deborah L. Madsen. In addition to an analysis of Kickapoo artist Arigon Starr's *Super Indian* (which I will also discuss in chapter 1),

Bernardin also discusses Starr's cofounding in 2011 (with Laguna Pueblo artist and educator Dr. Lee Francis IV) of "INC: the Indigenous Narratives Collective, a comics creation, publication, and distribution venture" (488). Bernardin's article also includes a discussion of digital media—video games as well as digital comics, such as *Super Indian*—and, as such, is a fantastic starting point for readers interested in Indigenous popular culture.

11. All that said, we can also understand Indigenous authors' work outside of the major publishing houses as a political act, whereby Indigenous comics artists are engaged in a radical refusal to "sell out" to an industry that for years has worked to erase Indigenous peoples, either through absence or through the use of harmful stereotypes. Indigenous authors could be understood as akin to the situation in academia that Leanne Betasamosake Simpson (2017; Mississauga Nishnaabeg) alludes to in *As We Have Always Done: Indigenous Freedom through Radical Resistance,* when she argues, "The thing for Nishnaabeg [and, by implication, other Indigenous peoples] to do is to stop looking for legitimacy within the colonizer's education system and return to valuing and recognizing our own individual and collective intelligence on its own merits and on our own terms" (171). Native Realities Press, noted above, can be understood as one such outlet, circumventing major publishers to distribute Indigenous comics artists. However, given the material reality of publishing and distribution, we are likely many years away from Native Realities being able to meaningfully compete with such powerhouses as Marvel and DC, though they may very well carve out the kind of space created by smaller publishers such as Top Shelf Productions.

12. To give one salient example, Theo Tso—creator of the superhero series *Captain Paiute* (discussed in chapter 1)—has more than once posted to his social media accounts the names and locations of the bookstores that he was bringing copies of his latest issues to. In addition to making sure his books are available for sale, Tso is ensuring that potential readers have the opportunity to see Indigenous art produced by Indigenous artists available for sale. This is similar to what Derek Lackaff and Michael Sales (2013) have noted for Black comics artists: "Over the last few years, [Rich] Watson and others have taken advantage of the new social media to cultivate relationships and communities, inform and educate comix readers, and explore new models for developing Black comic art" (65).

13. In his excellent study *Native Americans in Comic Books*, Michael A. Sheyahshe (2008; Caddo) outlines and provides detailed readings of several such stereotypes that have been used to characterize Indigenous peoples, including (but not limited to): "the *Mohican Syndrome*, in which a white man becomes Indian" (13); the "hero with ancestry from two cultures" (28); "the Indian as sidekick" (39); and "instant shaman" (55). He concludes his book, by noting, "With some artistic control from Indigenous writers and artists, comic books may offer a less narrow view of Native

Americans" (192–93). Sheyahshe has worked as a writer as well as a scholar in this field, as we will see in his story "Xenesi: The Traveler," discussed in chapter 2.

14. In his study *Deep Waters: The Textual Continuum in American Indian Literature*, Christopher B. Teuton (2010) follows a similar line of thinking when he argues that Native American literature "continues a sophisticated critical practice that explores the roles of the individual and the community in the context of survivance, balance, harmony, and peace, among other tribally specific values" (xv). Although Teuton focuses on the long-standing "preoccupation" (xix) in Indigenous literary studies that splits written works from oral works (6–7), his choice of wording—the "juxtaposing [of] oral and *graphic* forms of expression" (xix; emphasis added)— suggests that Indigenous comics art is a fruitful area of study that highlights how limiting this division has been, especially given his later claim that "there are forms of representing and referencing experience that are not well served by writing as recorded speech" (13).

15. This is an actual argument I had with my friend Ethan Shantie. After what seemed like hours of debate, we came to no clear answer.

16. And while genre expectations can be productive in meaning making, they can also cause confusion among the audience. Take, for example, the TV show *Legion*, which ran on FX for three seasons (2017–2019). Named for the superhero identity of the show's main character, David Haller, *Legion* took place in the larger X-Men cinematic universe (much in the same way that the ABC program *Agents of SHIELD* was part of the larger Marvel Cinematic Universe). However, Legion himself is not a member of the X-Men, and the show did not bring in any of the familiar X-Men characters until the third season, when David's father, Charles Xavier (Prof. X), was brought into the show. Eschewing the more familiar tropes of superhero narratives—such as costumed heroes battling nefarious evildoers—*Legion* did not enjoy the popularity of the larger cinematic franchise, despite many rave reviews by critics. While there are certainly many factors at play, one reason for its comparatively low ratings is surely its refusal to play into typical genre conventions for "superhero narratives" generally and clear connections to the X-Men cinematic universe more specifically. Fans of the X-Men franchise found a narrative wholly unlike what they would have expected based on the movies (in terms of narrative structure, character development, cinematography, etc.). And while some fans (such as myself) found the departure refreshing—I think it's one of the best-produced and most innovative TV programs in recent years—others were surely turned off by its refusal to fulfill genre-based expectations.

17. That said, as Eric Gary Anderson (2020) writes about speculative fiction (or what is often called "genre fiction") more broadly, "these recent, flourishing, genre-minded configurations of Native American fiction do not emerge from a literary vacuum but stand in experimentally traditional and traditionally experimental

relation to a host of precursors" (433). Just as Anderson develops the linkages between classics of the (so-called) "Native American Renaissance" and the emerging works of Indigenous speculative fiction, we should read Indigenous comics as participating both in the multifaceted traditions of Indigenous literature(s) as well as the complex history of graphic narrtive(s).

18. In his study *The Political Arrays of American Indian Literary History*, James H. Cox (2019) reminds us that "no form or genre emerges as more conservative or progressive than another" (3), and we would do well to remember that here. That is to say, the plasticity of genres allows for them to be vehicles for a wide array of political positions; even a quick survey of science fiction, for example, would yield politically conservative as well as politically progressive visions of the future and uses of advanced technology. And while I recognize the risk I run in contributing to Cox's fear that "literary critics risk missing both full artistic expression of Indigenous political life and all the intellectual, emotional, and communal labor required to navigate the politics of tribal national and settler-colonial worlds" (212), I do believe in the value of focusing on comics that—in various ways—engage a specific (if broadly defined) political position: challenges to the machinery of settler colonialism. This is not to say that all Indigenous comics do—or even should—perform such work. I hope that scholars continue to study the myriad political and aesthetic dimensions of Indigenous comics, especially those with political orientations that differ from those I discuss below.

CHAPTER 1. SUPER PROBLEMS REQUIRE SUPER HEROES: INDIGENOUS SUPERHEROES AND THEIR COMMUNITIES

1. In 2020, Marvel published the first volume of a new series, *Indigenous Voices*, featuring rebooted versions of Indigenous heroes in the Marvel universe. However, unlike past iterations of such characters as Echo, Mirage, and Moonstar, these characters are used in stories written and illustrated by Indigenous comics artists. The first issue featured the work of Jeffrey Veregge (Port Gamble S'Klallam), Weshoyot Alvitre (Tongva), Darcie Little Badger (Apache), Stephen Graham Jones (Blackfeet), and David Cutler (Mi'kmaq). I opt not to include these works in this chapter for a few reasons, the most important of which is my desire to highlight the work of artists publishing outside of the Marvel publishing powerhouse. Second, many of the superheroes included in *Indigenous Voices*—as well as the subsequent (and more expansive) *Marvel Voices: Heritage* published in 2022—are rebooted versions of existing Marvel characters. And while these rebooted characters are wonderfully reimagined—and engage in some of the same political work discussed below—I choose to focus exclusively on characters created by Indigenous artists.

It is refreshing to see Marvel employ Indigenous artists to help ensure that these existing characters are not used as racial stereotypes, and I am sure many readers are curious to see if and how these are eventually integrated into the larger Marvel Cinematic Universe. In a similar vein, I would like to draw attention to Daniel H. Wilson's work on the Earth 2 series for DC comics. A Cherokee science fiction writer perhaps most famous for his novels *Robopocalypse* and *Robogenesis*, Wilson also authored some of the titles in the *World's End, Society*, and *Future's End* series. However, none of these series focus on Indigenous heroes.

2. As Chris Gavaler (2018) points out, technically, only Marvel and DC employ "superheroes" as they "have maintained a jointly owned registered trademark on the word 'superhero' since 1979" (2). He also notes that "the history of the superhero is largely a history of DC and Marvel" (3). Indigenous creators are largely working outside of these larger publishing houses through smaller publishers. However, Native Realities Press (n.d.) is publishing works created by Indigenous comics artists, including reprinting Jon Proudstar's 1996 comic *Tribal Force*, which I will discuss briefly later in this chapter.

3. González (2017) quotes at length an interview with Frank Espinosa, author of *Rocketo*, which ends with the following: "We as Hispanics, as African Americans, as any minority, can write the new *Lord of the Rings*, the new *Star Wars*, the new *Harry Potters*, but if all we do is talk about one experience in our lives, we will remain trapped" (110).

4. Although Hillary Chute (2017) suggests that contemporary superhero comics are more "about failure and antiheroic figures" and "might be called anti-superheroic" (75), the persistence of traditional superheroes—especially in the larger media landscape, including film and television—cannot be denied.

5. In some of the early advertising for the 2017 superhero movie *Justice League*, DC employed logos to stand in for the characters themselves: Superman, Batman, Wonder Woman, the Flash, Aquaman, and Cyborg.

6. As Barbara Brownie and Danny Graydon (2016) note in their study *The Superhero Costume*, many costumes also work to position superheroes as "national personifications" (55), thus emphasizing the national identity of heroes even while their individual identities remain secret. Most recognizable, perhaps, is Captain America's flag-based costume, reminiscent of the flag-based elements found in the figure of Uncle Sam (and both characters have been used to recruit for the US military). While such figures are intended to be unambiguously patriotic, many Indigenous readers may rightly associate such figures with the continued colonization of North America by settler-colonial forces. Space prohibits a detailed discussion of reservation politics, but suffice to say that many reservation communities do not identify as American (or Canadian) and see the US (and Canadian) governments as overtly hostile forces. We see an example of such hostility on the opening page of *Captain Paiute* (figure 1.1).

7. Marvel's 2018 film *Black Panther* stands out as a counterexample that proves the rule. Although tied into the larger Marvel Cinematic Universe, Black Panther's primary concern is the protection of his nation Wakanda but not from any direct international or intergalactic threat (even if he was included as a hero in the following Avengers movie, *Infinity War*, fighting the alien threat Thanos). There is a case to be made that the nonwhite superheroes—Luke Cage as well as Black Panther—in the MCU are more focused on local community than their white counterparts. However, I do not have the space here to flesh out such an analysis.

8. Most of the comics under discussion have no page numbers. Page numbers will be denoted as "n.p. [#]." The number itself will refer to the page number as counted out from the first page of the narrative text, not including paratextual materials, prefatory or introductory material, etc. Quotations from prefatory or introductory materials will be noted with roman numerals, starting the count from the first page of the publication.

9. This was an omnibus bill that covered a variety of topics, including an overhaul of the Navigable Waters Protection Act of 1882. First Nations, Métis, and Inuit peoples opposed this bill (which, sadly, was passed) in an effort to protect their treaty rights in general and preserve their waterways specifically. Since 2012, the movement has grown to encompass numerous concerns related to Indigenous rights throughout Canada.

10. Paradigmatic examples include such pairs as Professor X and Magneto as well as Wolverine and Sabertooth from the *X-Men* series, Batman and Two-Face, and some versions of Superman and Lex Luthor. Williams returns as the villain for issue 2, which concludes with Captain Paiute driving the *anup'its* ("evil entity") from his former friend (Tso 2019, n.p. 22). And in true serial comic book fashion, the episode ends with the hero wondering if Williams is "cured for good, or . . ." (n.p. 24), promising a continuation of their enmity, potentially setting up Williams as the series' main antagonist.

11. As Adilifu Nama (2011) argues in his study *Super Black: American Pop Culture and Black Superheroes*, "As fantastic, imaginary, and speculative as superheroes are, once they engage real social events that clearly resonate as oppressive and unjust their actions or inactions become a cause of moral scrutiny because the superhero archetype is heavily steeped in affirming a division between right and wrong." Nama thus finds fault with the Black superhero Icon, a Superman-like figure who crash landed on Earth during slavery and did not "use his superior abilities to free black folk from enslavement" (96). In this regard, it is refreshing to see *Captain Paiute* clearly situate itself with respect to broader race-based civil rights issues, thus highlighting the series' commitment to social justice rather than using social justice issues as merely setting for superhero adventures. (That said, *Icon* does tackle inner-city poverty and gang violence, even while it uses American slavery as little more than an emotional backstory.)

12. Although I will only be working with the print volumes, readers can also follow *Super Indian* online at Starrwatcher Online (n.d.), where Starr also publishes new stories before they come out in print. The internet offers wonderful possibilities for Indigenous creators to share their work with a large and diverse audience.

13. Starr writes elsewhere that she "wanted to break the stereotype of the stoic, loner Indian that is persistent in mainstream Native stories. My hero would be a guy who had both parents (unlike Superman or Batman), lived in his community, and had friends within that community" (qtd. in Bernardin 2015, 485). In many ways, *Super Indian* challenges stereotypes of mainstream superheroes as well as Indigenous peoples.

14. The interested reader is also directed to Vizenor's (1992) essay "Ishi Bares His Chest: Tribal Simulations and Survivance" in the collection *Partial Recall: Photographs of Native North Americans*. Photographs of Indigenous peoples by others provide another fruitful area of study for the phenomenon of Indigenous peoples "under glass" in terms of the camera lens.

15. Anthropologists have long been a popular target for Indigenous writers, as figures who aptly represent a variety of interests—personal, professional, colonial— that have kept Indigenous peoples oppressed in North America. One of the most biting critiques of the anthropological study of Indigenous peoples was penned by Vine Deloria Jr. (1988), who writes, in *Custer Died for Your Sins: An Indian Manifesto*, that "behind each policy and program with which Indians are plagued, if traced completely back to its origin, stands the anthropologist" (81).

16. In an interview for *Dreaming in Indian*, Starr (2019) is asked, "Superman or Batman? Why?" While this question seems to be asking for her personal preference— a question of which classic superhero she finds more intriguing and why—her answer may also suggest why Super Indian is loosely modeled after the Man of Steel: "Superman . . . because he's a stranger in a strange land. Much like Native people are these days" (59).

17. In the novel from which this movie was adapted, Lieutenant Dunbar becomes champion for the Comanche; the alteration suggests that the Indigenous communities themselves are secondary to the importance of the white savior figure.

18. While Odjick is credited with work on the story, pencils, letters, colors, and inks for much of this book, he also worked with fellow Kitigan Zibi Anishinabe artist Patrick Tenascon on the story and inks, as well as artists Matt Austin and Ross Hughes for inks and colors on select pages.

19. Wisakedjak is the name of a traditional trickster figure in Anishinabe legend. He is often known in English as Whisky Jack, which is also the common name for the gray jay, a bird indigenous to the boreal forests of North America.

20. There is no mention of another identity or any life outside of his role as a superhero. That said, the "secret identity" is not a strict requirement, especially given

the many superheroes who operate under their given name, such as Dr. Strange and Luke Cage, or otherworldly figures, like Thor.

21. I have written about Indigenous comics responses to this problem elsewhere; I direct the interested reader to "Graphic (Narrative) Presentations of Violence against Indigenous Women: Responses to the MMIW Crisis in North America" (Donahue 2020a).

22. Proudstar (2019) uses Thunder Eagle again in "Slave Killer," his contribution to *Moonshot*, volume 3. Set in the past—"a time before the white man" (20)—Thunder Eagle "was dispatched to this world to end Tsonokwa's evil ways" (21), after Tsonokwa's killing and enslaving of others. Not exactly a traditional superhero backstory, this vignette does provide an interesting addition to the mythology of Thunder Eagle and is hopefully the first of many more stories featuring this exciting hero.

23. Jones is listed as both writer and creator of this book, though he worked with multimedia visual artist Aaron Lovett as illustrator, with letters provided by Sulac, Kathryn S. Renta, and Joshua Viola. Because he is specifically listed as "creator," all artistic decisions will be attributed to Jones as creative lead, recognizing that the visual art is a collaborative effort among the previously named artists.

24. Silly names created by forcing two words together seems to be a common trope among fan creations. I myself did the very same thing when, in high school, I entered a contest to design a new superhero. My own failed offering was a hero known as "the Manimal," a man who could transform into any animal.

25. Frederick Aldama (2017) argues that "DC and Marvel superhero storyworlds rely heavily on the geometrizing of story as the dominant element at play in our cocreating activities. It is this skillful and willful visualizing—*geometrizing*—of character, theme, and plot that guides our gap-filling processes and shapes our experiences of a given comic book" (94). Jones's work can thus be read as an apt literalization of Aldama's metaphor that helps readers better understand the mechanics of the cocreative act.

26. These disparities should not be read as poor storytelling or sloppy editing; rather, we should read this comic as a work in progress, one in which the reader is invited to engage as part of the "cocreative act" Aldama identifies.

27. Although not specifically presented as a "superhero" narrative, "Changing Woman," written and illustrated by Shaun Beyale (2019; Navajo), employs superhero tropes to reimagine the story of Changing Woman (Asdzáá Naadleehi), one of the creation spirits and a figure of transformative power. Creator of *Ayla: The Monster Slayer*, a superhero comic currently under development (as of this writing), Beyale draws Changing Woman as one would a superhero, flying through space and emitting power blasts from her hands (21), closing the story with a full page representation of her in a classic "superhero pose," inviting her grandchildren (as well as the reader) to "help me bring balance back to the future" (24). As a time-travelling "superhero," who

also appears to travel through outer space to fight evil (21), Changing Woman serves as an interesting linchpin between superhero comics and science fiction comics, which I will address in the next chapter. For more on Beyale and his forthcoming comic, see Locke 2018.

28. Author of *Antifa: The Anti-Fascist Handbook* and *Translating Anarchy: The Anarchism of Occupy Wall Street,* Bray is an active antifascist organizer and member of the faculty of the Gender Research Institute at Dartmouth (GRID).

29. In 2017, Bray became the subject of much discussion in the media and online when—on an episode of *Meet the Press*—he noted that "when pushed, self-defense is a legitimate response to white supremacist and neo-Nazi violence" (qtd. in Hawkins 2017, n.p.).

CHAPTER 2. INDIGENOUS TRAVELS IN SPACE, TIME, AND TECHNOLOGY

1. In my research for this chapter, I learned that both of these franchises have a rich history in Indigenous arts and serve as a touchstone for many scholars' discussions of Indigenous futurism. As one example, I would point to Yvonne N. Tiger's (2019) use of Star Trek as her example (and contemporary reference point) for "non-interventionist, patriarchal settler-colonialism hurtling through the universe" (146). Her article also provides a fascinating study of the first *Moonshot* volume and the ways various Indigenous comics creators retell traditional stories through Indigenous futurism. Additionally, I learned through Suzanne Newman Fricke's (2019) introduction to the fantastic issue of *World Art* devoted to Indigenous futurisms that "the first movie dubbed into Diné (Navajo) was *Star Wars: A New Hope*. Released in 2013, this version was part of an effort to encourage fluency in Diné, especially for children" (108).

2. The one notable exception from a major science fiction franchise is the character of Chakotay, first officer of the *USS Voyager* in the *Star Trek* franchise (*Star Trek: Voyager* ran for seven seasons on the UPN network and was the fifth series in the *Star Trek* franchise). Not given a specific tribal identity, the character's heritage was addressed in the episode "Tattoo" (season 2, episode 9), where he came to appreciate his (unnamed) cultural heritage through visions of the past that connect his ancestors with a charge of environmental stewardship. Many critics and fans complained about Chakotay's character, with Sierra S. Adare (2005) calling him the "quintessential Tonto for outer space" (95); Robert Beltran, the Mexican American actor who portrayed the character, even notes that he was "continually positioned as an exotic native other in relation to the white female Captain Janeway" (qtd. in Geraghty 2009, 72). As Christine Morris reminds us from her 1979 article on portrayals of Native Americans in popular science fiction, the *Star Trek* franchise has

long employed stereotypes. In the *Star Trek* (original series) episode "The Paradise Syndrome" (season 3, episode 3), for instance, Morris (1979) identifies the key tropes of the "idealized portrayal of Indian peoples" (301), including "childlike tribal peoples," the "beautiful Indian Princess," and the "technologically superior white man and his sidekick" (302). One could argue that such stereotypes are as integral to science fiction as they are to westerns.

3. One notable exception in comics is the series *East of West* (2013–2019), created by Jonathan Hickman and Nick Dragotta. In this series, Indigenous peoples belong to the Endless Nation, one of the six nations in an alternate-universe United States where the Civil War never ended. The Endless Nation is the most technologically advanced of the six nations, possessing personal and military technologies far more advanced than those of their contemporaries.

4. Additionally, I should also note that "Indigenous futurism" encompasses much more than merely representations of and engagements with a "future" or a period of time that has not yet come to pass. As Suzanne Newman Fricke (2019) notes, "the term suggests a time outside of the timeline we are in. It could even refer to the past, to a re-envisioning of what has already happened" (116). This chapter presents just one piece of the larger mosaic of Indigenous futurism. The reader could productively read chapter 3 of this book, on historical narratives, as part of that larger mosaic (even though I do not present it as such in the chapter itself).

5. And to be sure, there are Indigenous authors producing such work, although mostly in traditional novels. This growing list includes such works as Misha's (sadly, out-of-print) novel *Red Spider White Web* (1990) and much of Daniel H. Wilson's body of work, especially *Robopocalypse* (2011) and *Robogenesis* (2014).

6. Lavender should be commended for including essays devoted to Indigenous literature in this collection (see Lavender 2014a). That said, Patrick B. Sharp's (2014) essay "Questing for an Indigenous Future: Leslie Marmon Silko's *Ceremony* as Indigenous Science Fiction" compellingly highlights the absence of Indigenous narratives in the literature of science fiction. Personally, I find his analysis of "Silko's use of generic elements common to science fiction" (120) to be a bit thin, but I commend him for drawing attention to the idea that Indigenous science fiction has been hiding in plain sight.

7. I would like to direct the reader interested in the study of race as a structural component of narrative to my coedited collection *Narrative, Race, and Ethnicity in the United States* (Donahue, Ho, and Morgan 2017).

8. As of this writing, there are a number of people complaining about the ways in which the media (narrative media as well as news media) "politicizes" race. One popular refrain is that the media needs to return to an apolitical past when politics—especially the politics of race—were ignored. Of course, no such time existed, as scholars like Kilgore and those writing in his wake demonstrate. That

said, we should remember that, while science fiction has always been political, it has not always been progressive. As Kilgore (2003) again reminds us, "Contemporary astrofuturists fall along a political spectrum that ranges from Jerry Pournelle on the right, offering readers a neoclassical, space-based Empire of Man that escapes the democratization of mid-twentieth-century America, to Vonda N. McIntyre and Kim Stanley Robinson on the left, whose struggles to articulate the conventions of imperial exploration with a left-egalitarian politics have resulted in genre-bending thought experiments" (2).

9. I have addressed this issue in contemporary historical fiction of the American frontier in my book *Failed Frontiersmen: White Men and Myth in the Post-Sixties American Historical Romance* (Donahue 2015). Far too often, even well-meaning scholars take a default position in uncritically using "the American dream" as a metaphor for progress. Unfortunately, Kilgore's (2003) only discussion of Indigenous peoples in his study comes in his analysis of Ben Bova's 1999 novel *Return to Mars*, in which "Bova offers the various Indians and indigenous peoples of the Earth a chance to be history's winners, and that is no small accomplishment" (221). In addition to using the work of a white writer to explore Indigenous issues, Kilgore also uncritically suggests that "Indigenous peoples" should be considered history's losers, completely dismissing their powerful acts of survivance as well as their possible contributions to the future, which many Indigenous science fiction writers explore, as we will see below. (Additionally, his section titled "Red Man on a Red Planet" [212] demonstrates a reliance on racial stereotyping that he is all too willing to employ for a cheap rhetorical gesture.)

10. As demonstrated in the following chapter on historical comics—as well as more generally in Indigenous narrative literature—many Indigenous authors reject the Western notion of strict chronological time and work to demonstrate the fluidity of—if not the strict contiguity of—such notions as past, present, and future, rejecting what Mark Rifkin (2017) calls "settler time" in his study *Beyond Settler Time: Temporal Sovereignty and Indigenous Self-Determination*.

11. Though it should perhaps go without saying, my comments are not limited to comics and graphic novels. There is a rapidly growing body of work in Indigenous science fiction, including works by Cherie Dimaline (Métis), Daniel H. Wilson (Cherokee), Stephen Graham Jones (Blackfeet), and others. *Encountering the Sovereign Other: Indigenous Science Fiction*, by Miriam C. Brown Spiers (2021) is a wonderful recent study that serves as a fantastic introduction to some of the more prominent authors.

12. It should be noted that a variety of marginalized groups have turned to futurisms for political expression. In her study of queer speculative fiction from 1890–2010, *Old Futures: Speculative Fiction and Queer Possibility*, Alexis Lothian (2018) explores "what imagined futures mean for those *away from whom* futurity

is distributed: oppressed populations and deviant individuals, who were denied access to the future by dominant imaginaries, but who work against oppression by dreaming of new possibility" (4–5; emphasis original).

13. Dillon (2014a) repeats this point in her essay "Haint Stories Rooted in Conjure Science: Indigenous Scientific Literacies in Andrea Hairston's *Redwood and Wildfire*," included in Lavender's collection *Black and Brown Planets: The Politics of Race in Science Fiction*: "conjuring" is "a native science" that includes "quantum mechanics and organic physics" (107); or more directly, "conjuring is a science" (113). It should be noted that Hairston herself is an African American author whose award-winning novel engaged Indigenous science as part of its speculative worldbuilding.

14. There has been some public debate about Roanhorse's identification as part of the Ohkay Owingeh Pueblo people. Although much of her early work notes her tribal identification, recent work does not. Readers interested in this ongoing discussion can productively start their reading with Acee Agoyo's (2020; Pueblo) thoughtful article "'The Elizabeth Warren of the Sci-Fi Set': Author Faces Criticism for Repeated Use of Tribal Traditions."

15. Many Indigenous creators have made similar comments. In an interview with Grace L. Dillon (2014b), Stephen Graham Jones, himself a comic artist as well as a novelist, states, "The future stories that deal with Indian stuff that I find most authentic, finally, are those that are informed by the past" (212). His superhero comic *My Hero* was discussed in the previous chapter.

16. I would like to thank an early reviewer for drawing my attention to Roanhorse's use of the phrase "zombie apocalypse," which Roanhorse drew from Dr. Cutcha Risling Baldy's (2013; Hoopa Valley Tribe) wonderful blog post "On Telling Native People to Just 'Get Over It' or Why I Teach about the Walking Dead in my Native Studies Classes. . . *Spoiler Alert!*" Readers interested in Indigenous politics and popular culture are invited to begin their reading here.

17. Although he admits to not being "particularly drawn to post-apocalyptic fiction. . . . Apocalypse doesn't interest me" (167), Daniel Heath Justice (2018) does briefly address the genre in his study *Why Indigenous Literatures Matter*, noting that "it's vital to remember that when Indigenous writers and other writers of colour imagine apocalypse, they think about what endures *beyond* it" (167). Even scholars largely disinterested in postapocalyptic writing recognize its growing importance in Indigenous studies, as well as its political importance as an apt vehicle for survivance narratives.

18. This seeming paradox is not unique to Indigenous futurism. Although I don't have the space here to fully develop the connections between contemporary race-based futurisms and their roots in the early twentieth-century futurisms developed in Europe, I would like to quote Vivien Greene (2014) who, in the "Introduction" to her collection *Italian Futurism: 1909–1944*, notes, "Futurism was also a movement

punctuated by paradoxes" (21). In an essay in that same collection, Claudia Salaris (2014) notes, "Futurism arose against the background of profound economic, social, and cultural upheavals that marked the advent of modern, industrialized, urbanized society" (22). Though not at all considering Indigenous futurisms of the late twentieth to early twenty-first centuries, this statement absolutely characterizes this movement as well, aptly drawing a parallel between these two as-yet-unconnected aesthetic and political developments.

19. Also known as Richard Paul Davis, Crowsong notes that while he does "identify as Native American," he does not want to "use my heritage to sell books" (Davis, n.d., n.p.). I have not been able to identify his tribal affiliation from any of his publications or social-media outlets. Nor, however, is it necessary for him to so identify for his audience. I only note this because I have consistently identified the tribal affiliation for other artists and scholars in this book and do not want this lack of attribution to appear as an oversight.

20. The *Moonshot* collections also include a wide variety of narratives, in a number of genres, addressing various themes. For the purpose of this chapter, however, I will focus exclusively on science fiction.

21. Readers interested in graphic narratives involving the trickster figure should check out the award-winning collection *Trickster: Native American Tales; A Graphic Collection*, edited by Matt Dembicki (2010).

22. Primarily a visual artist whose work includes cover art for various comic-book titles (including such titles as *Red Wolf* and *Judge Dredd*), Veregge's work has long blended S'Klallam imagery with Salish line work. As he notes on his webpage, his art is informed by his "lifetime love affair with comic books, toys, TV and film . . . blending them with my Native perspective" (Veregge, n.d.). Veregge's online portfolio shows this aesthetic style employed to represent such classic science fiction images as the Millennium Falcon (from the *Star Wars* franchise) and various popular comic-book figures, such as Superman, Batman, and Spider-Man.

23. In an interview for the collection *Dreaming in Indian*, Veregge (2019a) uses the popular *Star Trek* character Spock as a means to express his racial identity. Just as Spock is the child of human and Vulcan parents, Veregge is "of mixed heritage. My mom is Native (S'Klallam, Suquamish, and Duwamish) and my dad is French/German" (108).

24. As Lindsey Catherine Cornum (n.d.; Diné) argues, "We must not fall into the trap of colonial visions of outer space and the future" (n.p.). By the same token, we should also avoid reading narratives of exploration as inherently colonial enterprises, despite their long history as such.

25. This is not to say that all Indigenous narratives employ Indigenous characters; such a claim would be as incorrect as it is rooted in a simplistic racial determinism.

26. As we will see below, the incorporation of tribal languages in such works can be a profound political statement.

27. While this needlessly gendered line was rewritten for *Star Trek: The Next Generation*, both versions still retain the subtle reminder of settler colonialism, even for a franchise that has long been celebrated (and at times denounced) for its "political correctness." Most episodes/films show the crew of the Enterprise meeting various nonhuman races, even while the tagline suggests that the crew is traveling where "no man"/"no one" has gone before. That is to say, the various beings indigenous to these planets are not "people," as humans in the series understand the term.

28. Although not my explicit focus here, it should be clear that many Indigenous science fiction narratives also explicitly warn against continued ecological disruption. As journalist and activist Johnnie Jae (Otoe-Missouria/Choctaw) states:

> Unlike mainstream science fiction, where futurism is typically violent and values the advancement of technology over both nature and human beings, Indigenous sci-fi is the polar opposite. We imagine worlds where the advancement of technology doesn't disrupt or destroy ecosystems or the balance of power between humans and nature. Even in stories where we are exploring alien worlds, we think about how we can coexist with the life forms indigenous to that world. We think about the ways our cultures, languages, and everything that makes us who we are can be preserved and how they can evolve in these new worlds. (Roanhorse et al. 2017, n.p.)

For more on this topic, see Jeremy M. Carnes's (2020) "Deep Time and Vast Place: Visualizing Land/Water Relations across Time and Space."

29. As of this writing, the *Star Trek* franchise has produced five television series, two streaming series (with two more in production), thirteen motion pictures, one animated series (with two more in production), one series of shorts, and hundreds of novels, novelizations, and graphic novels/comics.

30. One of the crew members also casually mentions beading, thus placing traditional craft work on the same page where the advanced technology is introduced. As with Veregge above, Starr is suggesting that traditional arts and advanced technology are not mutually exclusive.

31. Crowsong Productions can now be found online at https://richardpauldavis.wordpress.com/.

32. In the comic, the attribution is given as follows: "pages 1–4 excerpted from *Rainy Mountain* by Robert Momaday" (Crowsong 2018, n.p. v).

33. In 2019, Conundrum Press released an omnibus edition of *Dakwäkãda Warriors* (see Pauls 2019). Unless otherwise noted, however, all references to the text will be to the original Moniker Press editions (Pauls 2016, 2017, 2018). In addition

to collecting all three issues, the omnibus edition includes a section titled "Dänk'e Futurism: Creating Dakwäkäda Warriors," which provides the historical and cultural background behind the creation of the comic as well as a series of "pinups" drawn by other artists (akin to alternate covers included in many comics).

CHAPTER 3. THE PAST IS PART OF THE PRESENT:
INDIGENOUS HISTORICAL GRAPHIC NARRATIVES

1. As has been true of every other chapter in this book, only a handful of authors and texts have been selected for this chapter. The focus presented here should be considered just one dimension of the kinds of texts being produced and not a description of the range of narratives that exist or a prescriptive formula for what kinds of narratives are worthy of being read and studied.

2. It should go without saying that we will also leave aside Lukács's understanding of "progress," rooted as it is in an Enlightenment ideology that proved harmful to Indigenous peoples in North America (and elsewhere). That said, readers are certainly encouraged to understand the ways that many Indigenous authors are using their work to explicitly call for a more compassionate and historically well-informed understanding of Indigenous peoples and cultures, an arguably more important marker of "progress" than one Lukács (and many of his intended readers) focuses on.

3. This is not to say that she does not recognize the importance of collective action. However, any collective action that may come as a response to narratives of historical atrocities must first begin with individual readers; it is individual readers, and not social classes, that read books and come to feel empathy.

4. Admittedly, one reason that I am highlighting the use of comics as a form of communication between Indigenous artists and non-Indigenous readers is because of my own position as a non-Indigenous reader and scholar of Indigenous works. Certainly, many of these works are also aimed at Indigenous readers who—for various reasons, including the continued efforts at erasing Indigenous histories from academic curricula—have not learned about these people and events (or have not learned the truth about them). I will not use my work to speak on behalf of Indigenous readers, though I would like to note here the importance of such work in academic studies that I hope will follow and improve upon my own.

5. Classic examples include such works as Leslie Marmon Silko's *Ceremony*, James Welch's *Fools Crow*, and much of Louise Erdrich's work, as well as the recent rise of Indigenous speculative fiction narratives such as Cherie Dimaline's *The Marrow Thieves*.

6. I have written about representations of Indigenous time as nonlinear elsewhere; the interested reader is directed to my chapter "Indigenous Time/Indigenous

Narratives: The Political Implications of Non-Linear Time in Contemporary Native Fiction" (Donahue 2022c).

7. The three pages included for analysis were all illustrated by Robertson's longtime collaborator Scott B. Henderson, who illustrated four volumes of this series. Andrew Lodwick illustrated *The Rebel—Gabriel Dumont*, and Wai Tien illustrated both *The Peacemaker—Thanadelthur* and *The Land of Os—John Ramsay*.

8. It's never made clear in the series if those first few pages were truly a dream or her first moment of temporal transportation. While the first three books have Echo falling asleep before her travels—where she has real, material interactions with the people and places—by the fourth book, she can travel back at will (more on this below).

9. The reader slowly comes to learn about Echo's family situation, as she does not live with her mother until volume 3, in which the reader learns of Echo and her guardian that "we're ready to have you home" (Vermette 2020, 4). (As of volume 4, the reason for the separation has not been explicitly noted.) But Echo's desire for a connection with her mother is clear throughout; in addition to the above conversation, Echo's iPod is always set to either "Mom's Old CDs" or "Mom's Playlist." That said, this desire for connection is relatively passive at first; listening to playlists is hardly an active means of connection to another person.

10. Readers interested in Métis history and comics should check out Chester Brown's (2003) *Louis Riel: A Comic-Strip Biography*, which includes a focus on Riel's role in the Red River Resistance.

11. Sharp-eyed readers will notice that when Echo signs her name to sign up for the bake sale, the name immediately above hers on the list is that of series writer Katherena Vermette (Vermette 2018, 14). This should not be read merely as a hip self-reference, but rather as a subtle reminder that Vermette is a proud and active member of her community.

12. This event is recounted in volume 4.

13. Henderson illustrated four of the seven Tales from Big Spirit books and has also frequently collaborated with Robertson on many of his other books.

14. The educational focus is central to the series, as well as the work of Highwater Press more generally. The press also publishes a teacher's guide for these books (see Ferguson 2014).

15. This is not to say that these historical figures are unknown. For instance, Pauline Johnson is a well-regarded poet, and Gabriel Dumont is a well-known Métis leader. Rather, these figures have arguably not been given their due in contemporary historical discourse.

16. Although the Tales from Big Spirit series may be his most explicit exploration of the persistence of the past in the present, Robertson (2012) uses this idea in other collaborations, most significantly in *7 Generations: A Plains Cree Saga*. Rather than

repeat my comments here, I would direct the reader to my chapter "Indigenous Time/Indigenous Narratives" (Donahue 2022c).

17. I do not wish to wade into the fictionality debate taking place in some circles of narrative theory, though I recognize that those theorists may take issue with my seemingly pat dismissal of a rich field of study. I would direct the interested reader to Dorrit Cohn's classic 1999 study *The Distinction of Fiction* as a fine start to this line of inquiry.

18. White is also considering such discursive modes as the chronicle, which do not concern us here. Part of White's (1987) argument in this essay is that two discursive modes—such as the chronicle and the narrative—can convey the same information, "but different meanings are produced" (42) by virtue of their being conveyed via different discursive modes. One question I do not take up in this chapter—but which is well worth its own study—is the way "different meanings are produced" by narratives told through comics versus those told through purely verbal textual media. As always, we should never lose sight of the importance of the media we are engaging and their formal possibilities/limitations.

19. The various contextual materials noted above help to serve this purpose as well while also reminding the reader that stories such as this have sadly been understudied and are not as well known among the general public as they should be. The larger erasure of Indigenous stories is, of course, a major impetus for the continued production of Indigenous historical novels, graphic or otherwise. Their rising popularity among readers attests to the growing interest among readers, Indigenous and otherwise.

20. The historical materials included in the physical and virtual exhibitions attest to the newsworthiness of the event at the time even while reminding readers that it quickly faded from the larger (national) consciousness.

CHAPTER 4. PUSHING THE BOUNDARIES OF REPRESENTATION: INDIGENOUS EXPERIMENTAL GRAPHIC NARRATIVE

1. I would like to note here a distinction between "experimental" and "alternative." Charles Hatfield (2005) notes the problem with "the persistent use of those admittedly imprecise and loaded terms, 'mainstream' and 'alternative' to distinguish between the various types of comics vying for fans' attention" (31). And one problem with this pair of terms is that they are often tied to modes of production rather than the formal characteristics of the narrative. For instance, where Art Spiegelman's *MAUS* certainly began its life as an "alternative" comic, it is now fully "mainstream" in that it is readily available in bookstores and regularly included on syllabi. However, I would argue that at no point was it "experimental," given that Spiegelman was working in

genres (memoir/biography) and modes (allegory) that were familiar to comic-book creators and readers alike.

2. *Jimmy Corrigan* has also won, among other accolades, an American Book Award, an Eisner Award (Special Award for Excellence in Presentation and Best Graphic Album of Previously Published Work), and the Angoulême Festival's Prize for Best Comic Book and Prix de la critique (2003), making it an international award-winning book. Martha Kuhlman (2018) also notes, "*Building Stories* is the logical extension of ideas Ware has been cultivating for years in the tiny paper models included in *Jimmy Corrigan* and the *ACME Novelty Library*" (520). However, that should not detract from our recognition of the experimental nature of Ware's later work.

3. Though not focusing explicitly on "experimental" works, I attempted to address this particular issue in my book *Contemporary Native Fiction: Toward a Narrative Poetics of Survivance* (Donahue 2019), in which I demonstrate how the formal tools of narrative theory can help us better understand the political dimensions of Native American (US) and First Nations (CA) literary fiction while simultaneously suggesting that a widening of the narratological canon to include such narratives advances the literary critical project of narrative theory.

4. It has also become commonplace to conflate "experimental" with "postmodern," especially in discussions of Indigenous literature, suggesting that if one merely employs devices common among established postmodern writers, one becomes "experimental." As such, "experimental" itself becomes a genre with identifiable markers.

5. For her full discussion of Stein's literary experimentation, the interested reader is directed to DeKoven's study *A Different Language: Gertrude Stein's Experimental Writing* (1983).

6. For a list of his recent talks, as well as a recording of his TED Talk, the interested reader is directed to his webpage (Michael Nicoll Yahgulanaas, n.d.-b).

7. Although there is likely much to be learned from reading his work against other comic art from North America that draws from manga, Yahgulanaas is not working within the history Simon Grennan outlines in "The Influence of Manga on the Graphic Novel." This may come, in part, from Yahgulanaas's own conscious avoidance of working in the "'anglophone' comics genre" (Grennan 2018, 320) that Grennan studies. That said, any discussion of manga influence on North American comic art would benefit from a discussion of Yahgulanaas, just as any discussion of North American comic art in general would benefit from the conscious inclusion of Indigenous creators.

8. The interested reader is also directed to *Old Growth: Michael Nicoll Yahgulanaas*, edited by Liz Park, for a very different approach to the development of Yahgulanaas's artistry and his specific work as an activist for local environmental issues and their

importance in larger discussions of global climate change. As we will see in the coda, all the artists discussed in this book can be productively analyzed through myriad lenses, and as readers and scholars, we would do well to attend to the various kinds of work being done by these amazing artists.

9. Yahgulanaas's first published graphic novel was the limited-print run *No Tankers, Tanks,* "produced in 1977 for the Islands Protection Society, which was established in 1974 by Haida and non-Indigenous activists to safeguard the archipelago's natural heritage from the devastating destruction caused by resource-extractive industries" (Levell 2016, 16). For my purposes here, I am only working with those books that can be used to chart the genesis and development of "Haida manga," as well as working with volumes that remain in print and are readily available. As with the work of many Indigenous comic-book creators, some of the work—especially early work—has never been widely available and may currently be unavailable.

10. Later reprintings of *A Tale of Two Shamans* now include the subtitle *A Haida Manga*, although that subtitle was not used for the original publication.

11. But I should point out, this does not necessarily include new cultural elements. Other than drawing on the broadly defined visual aesthetic, Yahgulanaas's work does not otherwise engage in or respond to manga storytelling. That said, Japan does hold a special place for Yahgulanaas, his family, and the larger Haida community. As he notes, "In historical times Japan was a refuge for Haida. In my own family we have stories of people working on ships, fur sealing ships, and actually abandoning ship and paddling off to Hokkaido to become integrated into Japanese society." He then positions Japan as favorable compared to North America: whereas "Haida men in Japan were treated like full people, like human beings," in North America, "there were things like Indian toilets, restrictions of theatre seating, certain cafes that we could and could not eat in" (qtd. in Levell 2016, 47).

12. Susan Bernardin (2020) also connects the formline to the story's setting, noting, "This fluid movement, much like the coastal setting for the story, directs its shifting meaning" (362).

13. Spiers (2014) also calls attention to Yahgulanaas's subtle use of the formline in character development: "A careful reader can tell that something is wrong by paying attention to Red's interaction with the formline: as the story progresses, he begins to manipulate the line rather than relying on it as a support system and natural feature of the world" (53–54).

14. In 2019, Yahgulanaas published a prequel to *Red* titled *Carpe Fin: A Haida Manga*. While this book does continue Yahgulanaas's engaging work with the formline (in addition to the other aesthetic aspects of "Haida manga"), it does not engage in the metatextual work discussed below. Dedicated to "the many who feel few and to the strong who think themselves weak" (Yahgulanaas 2019, n.p. v), *Carpe Fin* is every bit as political a work as *Red*, even if it does not engage in the full range of experimentation as his most famous work.

15. For an introduction to the narrative potential of painting (and other arts), the interested reader is directed to Werner Wolf's (2017) "Transmedial Narratology: Theoretical Foundations and Some Applications (Fiction, Single Pictures, Instrumental Music)," particularly his discussion of "a polyphase single picture," or what he also calls a "polyscenic stand-alone picture" (266).

16. And in a move that would no doubt appeal to his publisher, because the pages are printed on both sides, the reader interested in creating the larger Haida visual art must use two books to complete the mural.

17. As Perry Nodelman (2012) notes, such a mural was shown in 2010 at the Vancouver Art Gallery.

18. A note informs the reader that this mural exists in a private collection as a 66" × 72" wordless watercolor on paper. Should the readers remove the pages and construct their own version, theirs will include language—narrative text as well as character speech, sometimes in speech bubbles—that are not present in the original. It should also be pointed out that Ian M. Thom (2009) notes that Yahgulanaas "has always been interested in watercolour . . . in both small and larger scale works" (171), and he reprints several examples in his entry on Yahgulanaas in *Challenging Traditions: Contemporary First Nations Art of the Northwest*.

19. In her author's bio section for both of her books discussed below, harris identifies as "tribal" but does not otherwise specify her nation. That said, both books end with a full-page thanks to the "Coast Salish Nations," specifically mentioning the "Chowéthel, Spópetes, Sq'éwqel, Sts'a'ï:les, Temélhem, Th'ewá:lí, and Xwchí:yó:m" communities (e.g., harris 2017, n.p. 36). One of the reviewers for this book confirmed her identity and tribal affiliation, both of which I choose not to share in this book. As she chooses not to explicitly identify herself in her books, I will not publicly identify her here. I will say that the author belongs to a coastal tribal nation in British Columbia, Canada, and does important work for her community in addition to her work as a cutting-edge comic-book creator.

20. harris is listed as author and illustrator for both books. That said, harris also provides an extensive list (in both books) of acknowledgments for the various artists who contributed to the books, naming everyone from the materials artists (wood, metal, fabrics) and photographers to translators and cultural advisors. Also listed are the supporting industries whose work helped bring these books to completion, from the companies who manufactured the physical materials to the coffee shop that fed and caffeinated those involved in the project. As such, harris's acknowledgments highlight the larger communities involved with the completion of artistic projects, both directly and indirectly.

21. *The Brick Bible* was originally published under Spurling's birth name, Brendan Powell Smith. I owe a debt of gratitude to Gene Kannenberg Jr. for bringing this connection to my attention and introducing me to Spurling's work, examples of which can be found online (see The Brick Bible, n.d.).

22. One could also read harris's experimentation against the history of action figures, which have long been associated with comic books (especially superhero comics). Jonathan Alexandratos and Daniel F. Yezbick (2018) define action figures as the "companion objects that psychically and mythically reach out to us, . . . begging to place their bodies within the greater contexts of our experience and imagination" (102). In this reading, harris would almost be working in reverse, creating the "action figures" first, in order to serve the narrative.

23. Figure 4.8 shows the cast of *Blueberry Boy*, which includes one character (Tsek) who was created with face merging software. No information is given as to whose faces were used.

24. Michael A. Sheyahshe's (2008) groundbreaking study *Native Americans in Comic Books: A Critical Study* provides a thorough discussion of these stereotypes with examples.

25. Much has been written about Hollywood's problematic portrayal of Indigenous peoples; the reader interested in this topic will find Angela Aleiss's (2005) study *Making the White Man's Indian: Native Americans and Hollywood Movies* a useful starting point.

26. "The Sixties Scoop" refers to the practice in Canada of kidnapping—"scooping up"—First Nations, Inuit, and Métis children and placing them in foster homes. Despite its name, the practice began in the 1950s and persisted into the 1980s.

CODA: BUT WAIT, ISN'T THERE MORE?

1. In his introductory "Publisher's Note," Dr. Lee Francis IV (2016) notes, in his discussion of the code talkers, that "superheroes come in all shapes and sizes" (n.p.), and a compelling case could be made for including this book—and perhaps the various other war narratives—in a larger discussion of superhero comics.

2. This organizational method opens up even more possibilities if we study Indigenous comics and graphic novels alongside other narrative media, such as literary fiction or TV and movies. David A. Robertson and Stephen Graham Jones, for instance, are themselves also novelists. Other artists, like Jeffrey Veregge and Michael Nicoll Yahgulanaas, are noted installation artists. Arigon Starr is also an award-winning musician.

3. At least this is the case as represented by the recent titles and tables of contents of academic monographs. I am happy to report, however, that academic conferences have become hotspots of fascinating discussions about Indigenous comics and graphic novels. As I write this footnote, I hope that many of the wonderful papers on the subject are finding their way into edited collections or are adapted into chapters of monographs.

4. Bookstores like Red Planet Books, now ATCG Books and Comics (which is associated with Native Realities Press), and artists like Theo Tso have taken advantage of the wide reach offered by social media, with Facebook and Instagram accounts that boast thousands of followers and are rising.

REFERENCES

Adare, Sierra S. 2005. *"Indian" Stereotypes in TV Science Fiction: First Nations' Voices Speak Out*. Austin: University of Texas Press, 2005.

Agoyo, Acee. 2020. "'The Elizabeth Warren of the Sci-Fi Set': Author Faces Criticism for Repeated Use of Tribal Traditions." Indianz.com, June 24, 2020. https://www.indianz.com/News/2020/06/24/the-elizabeth-warren-of-the-scifi-set-au.asp.

Aldama, Frederick Luis. 2017. *Latinx Superheroes in Mainstream Comics*. Tuscon: University of Arizona Press.

Aldama, Frederick Luis, ed. 2020. *Graphic Indigeneity: Comics in the Americas and Australasia*. Jackson: University Press of Mississippi.

Aleiss, Angela. 2005. *Making the White Man's Indian: Native Americans and Hollywood Movies*. Westport, CT: Praeger Publishers.

Alexandratos, Jonathan, and Daniel F. Yezbick. 2018. "Articulate This! Critical Action Figure Studies and Material Culture." In *Comics Studies Here and Now*, edited by Frederick Luis Aldama, 102–20. New York: Routledge.

Allen, Paula Gunn. 1986. *The Sacred Hoop: Recovering the Feminine in American Indian Traditions*. Boston: Beacon Press.

Alternate History Comics Inc. n.d.-a. "MOONSHOT: The Indigenous Comics Collection." Kickstarter. https://www.kickstarter.com/projects/1350078939/moonshot-the-indigenous-comics-collection. Accessed July 6, 2020.

Alternate History Comics Inc. n.d.-b. "MOONSHOT The Indigenous Comics Collection VOLUME 3!" Kickstarter. https://www.kickstarter.com/projects/1350078939/moonshot-the-indigenous-comics-collection-volume-3. Accessed July 6, 2020.

Anderson, Eric Gary. 2020. "Native American Horror, Fantasy, and Speculative Fiction." In *The Cambridge History of Native American Literature*, edited by Melanie Benson Taylor, 431–46. Cambridge: Cambridge University Press.

Anderson, Reynaldo. 2015. "Critical Afrofuturism: A Case Study in Visual Rhetoric, Sequential Art, and Postapocalyptic Black Identity." In *The Blacker the Ink: Constructions of Black Identity in Comics and Sequential Art*, edited by Francis Gateward and John Jennings, 171–92. New Brunswick, NJ: Rutgers University Press, 2015.

Bailer, Bryn. 2014. "The First Comic Book with an All-Native American Superhero Team Returns: Conversation with Jon Proudstar about the Return of His Comic Book Series, 'Tribal Force.'" *Paonia High Country News*, February 17, 2014. https://www.hcn.org/issues/46.3/the-first-comic-book-with-an-all-native -american-superhero-team-returns.

Baldy, Cutcha Risling. 2013. "On Telling Native People to Just 'Get Over It' or Why I Teach about the Walking Dead in my Native Studies Classes. . . *Spoiler Alert!*" Cutcha Risling Baldy, PhD, December 11, 2013. http://www.cutcharislingbaldy .com/blog/on-telling-native-people-to-just-get-over-it-or-why-i-teach-about -the-walking-dead-in-my-native-studies-classes-spoiler-alert.

Bechdel, Alison. 2006. *Fun Home: A Family Tragicomic*. Boston: Mariner Books.

Berila, Beth. 2005. "Unsettling Calls for National Unity: The Pedagogy of Experimental Multiethnic Literatures." In "Pedagogy, Praxis, Politics, and Multiethnic Literatures," edited by Bonnie TuSmith and Sarika Chandra, special issue, *Multi-Ethnic Literature of the United States* 30, no. 2, (Summer): 31–47.

Bernardin, Susan. 2015. "Future Pasts: Comics, Graphic Novels, and Digital Media." In *The Routledge Companion to Native American Literature*, edited by Deborah L. Madsen, 480–93. London: Routledge.

Bernardin, Susan. 2020. "Afterlives: A Coda." In *Graphic Indigeneity: Comics in the Americas and Australasia*, edited by Frederick Luis Aldama, 361–63. Jackson: University Press of Mississippi.

Beyale, Shaun. 2019. "Changing Woman." In *Relational Constellation*, edited by Elizabeth LaPensée, 16–24. Vol. 2 of *Sovereign Traces*. East Lansing: Michigan State University Press.

Bray, Joe, Alison Gibbons, and Brian McHale. 2012. "Introduction." In *The Routledge Companion to Experimental Literature*, edited by Joe Bray, Alison Gibbons, and Brian McHale, 1–18. London: Routledge.

Bray, Mark. 2018. "Foreword." In *The Antifa Comic Book: 100 Years of Fascism and Antifa Movements*, by Gord Hill, 7–12. Vancouver, BC: Arsenal Pulp Press.

The Brick Bible. n.d. http://www.thebricktestament.com/. Accessed June 12, 2023.

Brooks, Lisa. 2012. "The Primacy of the Present, the Primacy of Place: Navigating the Spiral of History in the Digital World." *Publications of the Modern Language Association of America* 127, no. 2 (March): 308–16.

Brown, Chester. 2003. *Louis Riel: A Comic-Strip Biography*. Montreal, QC: Drawn & Quarterly.

Brown, Jeffrey A. 2020. "The Replacements: Ethnicity, Gender, and Legacy Heroes in Marvel Comics." In *The Oxford Handbook of Comic Book Studies*, edited by Frederick Luis Aldama, 387–401. Oxford: Oxford University Press.

Brownie, Barbara, and Danny Graydon. 2016. *The Superhero Costume: Identity and Disguise in Fact and Fiction*. London: Bloomsbury.

Bukatman, Scott. 2013. "A Song of the Urban Superhero." In *The Superhero Reader*, edited by Charles Hatfield, Jeet Heer, and Kent Worcester, 170–98. Jackson: University Press of Mississippi.

Carnes, Jeremy M. 2020. "Deep Time and Vast Place: Visualizing Land/Water Relations across Time and Space in *Moonshot: The Indigenous Comics Collection*." In *Graphic Indigeneity: Comics in the Americas and Australasia*, edited by Frederick Luis Aldama, 299–315. Jackson: University Press of Mississippi.

Carrington, André M. 2016. *Speculative Blackness: The Future of Race in Science Fiction*. Minneapolis: University of Minnesota Press.

Carsten, Cynthia. 2006. "*Storyteller*: Leslie Marmon Silko's Reappropriation of Native American History and Identity." *Wičazo Ša Review* 21, no. 2 (Autumn): 105–26.

Chute, Hillary. 2012. "Graphic Narrative." In *The Routledge Companion to Experimental Literature*, edited by Joe Bray, Alison Gibbons, and Brian McHale, 407–19. London: Routledge.

Chute, Hillary. 2017. *Why Comics? From Underground to Everywhere*. New York: HarperCollins.

Coogan, Peter. 2009. "The Definition of the Superhero." In *A Comics Studies Reader*, edited by Jeet Heer and Kent Worcester, 77–93. Jackson: University Press of Mississippi.

Cornum, Lindsey Catherine. n.d. "The Creation Story Is a Spaceship: Indigenous Futurism and Decolonial Deep Space." VOZ-À-VOZ / VOICE-À-VOICE. http://www.vozavoz.ca/feature/lindsay-catherine-cornum. Accessed September 23, 2021.

Cotter, Joshua W. 2009. *Driven by Lemons*. Richmond, VA: Adhouse Books.

Cox, James H. 2019. *The Political Arrays of American Indian Literary History*. Minneapolis: University of Minnesota Press.

Crowsong Productions. n.d. "Back Story." https://crowsong.net/the-s9-back-story. Accessed August 6, 2020.

Crowsong, Richard. 2018. *S9: Sequoyah 9*, no. 1. Edited by Cindy Lockwood, illustrated by Richard Crowsong, Derrick B. Lee, Tristan Oakenthorn, and Michael Waggoner. n.p.: Crowsong Productions.

Crowsong, Richard. 2019. "Sequoyah 9." Kickstarter, last updated May 17, 2019. https://www.kickstarter.com/projects/sq9/s9-the-comic-book.

Davis, Richard Crowsong. n.d. "Vile—The Legend of Thunder Valley." Indiegogo. https://www.indiegogo.com/projects/vile-the-legend-of-thunder-valley#/. Accessed August 6, 2020.

Deloria, Vine, Jr. 1988. *Custer Died for Your Sins: An Indian Manifesto*. Norman: University of Oklahoma Press.

Dembicki, Matt. 2010. *Trickster: Native American Tales; A Graphic Collection*. Golden, CO: Fulcrum.

Dillon, Grace L. 2012. "Imagining Indigenous Futurisms." In *Walking the Clouds: An Anthology of Indigenous Science Fiction*, edited by Grace L. Dillon, 1–12. Tucson: University of Arizona Press, 2012.

Dillon, Grace L. 2014a. "Haint Stories Rooted in Conjure Science: Indigenous Scientific Literacies in Andrea Hairston's *Redwood and Wildfire*." In *Black and Brown Planets: The Politics of Race in Science Fiction*, edited by Isiah Lavender III, 101–16. Jackson: University Press of Mississippi.

Dillon, Grace L. 2014b. "Imagining Indigenous Futurisms: An Interview with Stephen Graham Jones." *Paradoxa*, no. 26: 211–16.

Donahue, James J. 2015. *Failed Frontiersmen: White Men and Myth in the Post-Sixties American Historical Romance*. Charlottesville: University of Virginia Press.

Donahue, James J. 2019. *Contemporary Native Fiction: Toward a Narrative Poetics of Survivance*. New York: Routledge.

Donahue, James J. 2020a. "Graphic (Narrative) Presentations of Violence against Indigenous Women: Responses to the MMIW Crisis in North America." In *Routledge Companion to Gender and Sexuality in Comic Book Studies*, edited by Frederick Luis Aldama, 119–33. London: Routledge.

Donahue, James J. 2020b. "How Reading Shapes Us: James Donahue." Narrative Encounters, January 7, 2020. https://narrativeencounters.aau.at/how-reading -shapes-us-james-donahue/.

Donahue, James J. 2020c. "Indigenous Time/Indigenous Narratives: The Political Implications of Non-Linear Time in Contemporary Native Fiction." In *Ethnic American Literatures and Critical Race Narratology*, edited Alexa von Mossner, 15–31. New York: Routledge.

Donahue, James J., Jennifer Ho, and Shaun Morgan, eds. 2017. *Narrative, Race, and Ethnicity in the United States*. Columbus: Ohio State University Press.

Drawn & Quarterly. n.d. "A Brief History of Drawn & Quarterly." https://drawnand quarterly.com/about. Accessed September 13, 2020.

Duff, David. 2000. "Introduction." In *Modern Genre Theory*, edited by David Duff, 1–24. Essex: Longman.

Estes, Nick. 2019. *Our History Is the Future: Standing Rock versus the Dakota Access Pipeline, and the Long Tradition of Indigenous Resistance*. London: Verso.

Ferguson, Katya Adamov. 2014. *Teacher's Guide: For the Series Tales from Big Spirit*. Winnipeg, MB: Portage & Main Press.

Francis, Consuela. 2015. "American Truths: Blackness and the American Superhero." In *The Blacker the Ink: Constructions of Black Identity in Comics and Sequential Art*, edited by Frances Gateward and John Jennings, 137–52. New Brunswick: Rutgers University Press.

Francis, Lee, IV. 2016. "Publisher's Note." In *Tales of the Mighty Code Talkers*, edited by Arigon Starr, n.p. iv. Vol. 1. Albuquerque: Native Realities.

Francis, Lee, IV. 2019. *Ghost River: The Fall & Rise of the Conestoga.* Edited by Will Fenton, illustrated by Weshoyot Alvitre. Philadelphia: Library Company of Philadelphia.

Fricke, Suzanne Newman. 2019. "Introduction: Indigenous Futurisms in the Hyperpresent Now." *World Art* 9, no. 2: 107–21. https://doi.org/10.1080/21500 894.2019.1627674.

Frow, John. 2006. *Genre: The Critical Idiom.* London: Routledge.

Garroutte, Eva Marie. 2003. *Real Indians: Identity and the Survival of Native America.* Berkeley: University of California Press.

Gateward, Frances, and John Jennings. 2015. "Introduction: The Sweeter the Christmas." In *The Blacker the Ink: Constructions of Black Identity in Comics and Sequential Art*, edited by Frances Gateward and John Jennings, 1–15. New Brunswick: Rutgers University Press.

Gavaler, Chris. 2018. *Superhero Comics.* London: Bloomsbury.

Geraghty, Lincoln. 2009. *American Science Fiction Film and Television.* New York: Berg.

González, Christopher. 2017. *Permissible Narratives: The Promise of Latino/a Literature.* Columbus: Ohio State University Press.

Greene, Vivien. 2014. "Introduction." In *Italian Futurism: 1909–1944*, edited by Vivien Greene, 21. New York: Guggenheim Museum Publications.

Grennan, Simon. 2018. "The Influence of Manga on the Graphic Novel." In *The Cambridge History of the Graphic Novel*, edited by Jan Baetens, Hugo Frey, and Stephen E. Tabachnick, 320–36. Cambridge: Cambridge University Press.

harris, eelonqa K. 2017. *Nighthawk and Little Elk.* Agassiz, BC: TaleFeather.

harris, eelonqa K. 2018. *Blueberry Boy.* Agassiz, BC: TaleFeather.

Harris-Fain, Darren. 2018. "The Superhero Graphic Novel." In *The Cambridge History of the Graphic Novel*, edited by Jan Baetens, Hugo Frey, and Stephen E. Tabachnick, 492–508. Cambridge: Cambridge University Press.

Harrison, Richard. 2016. "Seeing and Nothingness: Michael Nicoll Yahgulanaas, Haida Manga, and a Critique of the Gutter." *Canadian Review of Comparative Literature/Revue Canadienne de Littérature Comparée* 43, no. 1 (March): 51–74.

Hatfield, Charles. 2005. *Alternative Comics: An Emerging Literature.* Jackson: University of Mississippi Press.

Hawkins, Derek. 2017. "A Dartmouth Antifa Expert Was Disavowed by His College President for 'Supporting Violent Protest,' Angering Many Faculty." *Washington Post*, August 29, 2017. https://www.washingtonpost.com/news/morning-mix/wp/2017/08/28/a-dartmouth-antifa-expert-was-disavowed-by-his-college -president-for-supporting-violent-protest-angering-many-faculty/?utm_ term=.60ceb034123a.

Herman, Matthew. 2010. *Politics and Aesthetics in Contemporary Native American Literature: Across Every Border.* New York: Routledge.

Hill, Gord. 2010. *The 500 Years of Resistance Comic Book.* Vancouver, BC: Arsenal Pulp Press.

Hill, Gord. 2012. *The Anti-Capitalist Resistance Comic Book.* Vancouver, BC: Arsenal Pulp Press.

Hill, Gord. 2018. *The Antifa Comic Book: 100 Years of Fascism and Antifa Movements.* Vancouver, BC: Arsenal Pulp Press.

Houseman, Todd. 2015. "Ayanisach." Illustrated by Ben Shannon. In *Moonshot: The Indigenous Comics Collection,* edited by Hope Nicholson, 131–38. Vol. 1. Toronto, ON: Alternate History Comics.

Jerng, Mark C. 2018. *Racial Worldmaking: The Power of Popular Fiction.* New York: Fordham University Press.

Jones, Stephen Graham. 2017. *My Hero.* Erie, CO: Hex.

Justice, Daniel Heath. 2018. *Why Indigenous Literatures Matter.* Waterloo, ON: Wilfred Laurier University Press.

Kelp-Stebbins, Katherine. 2020. "Reading Spaces: The Politics of Page Layout." In *The Oxford Handbook of Comic Book Studies,* edited by Frederick Luis Aldama, 75–93. Oxford: Oxford University Press.

Kilgore, DeWitt Douglas. 2003. *Astrofuturism: Science, Race, and Visions of Utopia in Space.* Philadelphia: University of Pennsylvania Press.

Kuhlman, Martha. 2018. "Reinvention of the Form: Chris Ware and Experimentalism after *Raw.*" In *The Cambridge History of the Graphic Novel,* edited by Jan Baetens, Hugo Frey, and Stephen E. Tabachnick, 509–25. Cambridge: Cambridge University Press.

Lackaff, Derek, and Michael Sales. 2013. "Black Comics and Social Media Economics: New Media, New Production Models." In *Black Comics: Politics of Race and Representation,* edited by Sheena C. Howard and Ronald L. Jackson II, 65–78. London: Bloomsbury.

Lavender, Isiah, III. 2011. *Race in American Science Fiction.* Bloomington: Indiana University Press.

Lavender, Isiah, III, ed. 2014a. *Black and Brown Planets: The Politics of Race in Science Fiction.* Jackson: University Press of Mississippi.

Lavender, Isiah, III. 2014b. "Introduction." In *Black and Brown Planets: The Politics of Race in Science Fictioni,* edited by Isiah Lavender III, 3–11. Jackson: University Press of Mississippi.

Levell, Nicola. 2016. *The Seriousness of Play: The Art of Michael Nicoll Yahgulanaas.* London: Black Dog.

Lincoln, Kenneth. 1983. *Native American Renaissance.* Berkeley: University of California Press.

Locke, Katherine. 2018. "Navajo Artist Creates Native Superheroes for New Comic Book." *Flagstaff Navajo-Hopi Observer*, July 31, 2018. https://www.nhonews.com/news/2018/jul/31/navajo-artist-creates-native-superheroes-new-comic/.

Lothian, Alexis. 2018. *Old Futures: Speculative Fiction and Queer Possibility*. New York: New York University Press.

Lowry, Chag. 2019. *Soldiers Unknown*. Illustrated by Rahsan Ekedal. Temecula, CA: Great Oak Press.

Luckhurst, Roger. 2005. *Science Fiction*. Cambridge, UK: Polity Press.

Lukács, Georg. 1983. *The Historical Novel*. Translated by Hannah Mitchell and Stanley Mitchell. Lincoln: University of Nebraska Press.

Michael Nicoll Yahgulanaas. n.d.-a. "Biography." https://mny.ca/en/biography/. Accessed June 11, 2023.

Michael Nicoll Yahgulanaas. n.d.-b. "Speaking." https://mny.ca/en/speaking/. Accessed June 11, 2023.

Morris, Christine. 1979. "Indians and Other Aliens: A Native American View of Science Fiction." *Extrapolation* 20, no. 4: 301–7.

Nama, Adilifu. 2011. *Super Black: American Pop Culture and Black Superheroes*. Austin: University of Texas Press.

Native Realities Press. n.d. https://atcgbooksandcomics.com/collections/native-realities-press. Accessed June 15, 2024.

Nodelman, Perry. 2012. "Picture Book Guy Looks at Comics: Structural Differences in Two Kinds of Visual Narrative." *Children's Literature Association Quarterly* 37, no. 4 (Winter): 436–44.

Odjick, Jay. 2010 *Kagagi: The Raven*. Illustrated, lettered, and penciled by Jay Odjick. Patrick Tenascon, Story, Inks. Coquitlam, BC: Arcana Comics, Inc.

Pauls, Cole. 2016. *Dakwäkãda Warriors in Sha Catcher*. Vancouver, BC: Moniker Press.

Pauls, Cole. 2017. *Dakwäkãda Warriors II*. Vancouver, BC: Moniker Press.

Pauls, Cole. 2018. *Dakwäkãda Warriors III*. Vancouver, BC: Moniker Press.

Pauls, Cole. 2019. *Dakwäkãda Warriors*. Gauvin, QC: Conundrum Press.

Polak, Kate. 2017. *Ethics in the Gutter: Empathy and Historical Fiction in Comics*. Columbus: Ohio State University Press.

Portage & Main Press. n.d. https://www.portageandmainpress.com/. Accessed June 25, 2023.

Proudstar, Jon. 2017. *Tribal Force*, no. 1. Colored and cover art illustrated by Weshoyot Alvitre, penciled and inked by Ron Joseph. Albuquerque: Native Realities.

Proudstar, Jon. 2019. "Slave Killer." Illustrated by David Cutler. In *Moonshot: The Indigenous Comics Collection*, edited by Elizabeth LaPensée and Michael Sheyahshe, 19–29. Vol. 3. Iqaluit, NU: Inhabit Education Books.

Red Planet Books & Comics. n.d. "About." https://redplanetbooksncomics.com/pages/about. Accessed September 15, 2020.

Rieder, John. 2008. *Colonialism and the Emergence of Science Fiction*. Middletown, CT: Wesleyan University Press.

Rifkin, Mark. 2017. *Beyond Settler Time: Temporal Sovereignty and Indigenous Self-Determination*. Durham, NC: Duke University Press.

Roanhorse, Rebecca. 2018. "Postcards from the Apocalypse." Uncanny: A Magazine of Science Fiction and Fantasy, 2018. https://uncannymagazine.com/article/postcards-from-the-apocalypse/.

Roanhorse, Rebecca, Elizabeth LaPensée, Johnnie Jae, and Darcie Little Badger. 2017. "Decolonizing Science Fiction and Imagining Futures: An Indigenous Futurisms Roundtable." *Strange Horizons*, January 30, 2017. http://strangehorizons.com/non-fiction/articles/decolonizing-science-fiction-and-imagining-futures-an-indigenous-futurisms-roundtable/.

Robertson, David Alexander. 2012. *7 Generations: A Plains Cree Saga*. Illustrated by Scott B. Henderson. Winnipeg, MB: Highwater Press.

Robertson, David Alexander. 2014a. *The Ballad of Nancy April—Shawnadithit*. Illustrated by Scott B. Henderson. Tales from Big Spirit 1. Winnipeg, MB: Highwater Press.

Robertson, David Alexander. 2014b. *The Land of Os—John Ramsay*. Illustrated by Wai Tien. Tales from Big Spirit 6. Winnipeg, MB: Highwater Press.

Robertson, David Alexander. 2014c. *The Peacemaker—Thanadelthur*. Illustrated by Wai Tien. Tales from Big Spirit 4. Winnipeg, MB: Highwater Press.

Robertson, David Alexander. 2014d. *The Poet—Pauline Johnson*. Illustrated by Scott B. Henderson. Tales from Big Spirit 5. Winnipeg, MB: Highwater Press.

Robertson, David Alexander. 2014e. *The Rebel—Gabriel Dumont*. Illustrated by Andrew Lodwick. Tales from Big Spirit 2. Winnipeg, MB: Highwater Press.

Robertson, David Alexander. 2014f. *The Scout—Tommy Prince*. Illustrated by Scott B. Henderson. Tales from Big Spirit 3. Winnipeg, MB: Highwater Press.

Robertson, David Alexander. 2016. *The Chief—Mistahimaskwa*. Illustrated by Scott B. Henderson. Tales from Big Spirit 7. Winnipeg, MB: Highwater Press.

Romagnoli, Alex S., and Gian S. Pagnucci. 2013. *Enter the Superheroes: American Values, Culture, and the Canon of Superhero Literature*. Lanham, MD: Scarecrow Press.

Salaris, Claudia. 2014. "The Invention of the Programmatic Avant-Garde." In *Italian Futurism: 1909–1944*, edited by Vivien Greene, 22–49. New York: Guggenheim Museum Publications.

Shaggy, Kayla. 2017. *The Sixth World*. n.p.: Triple Jeopardy Productions.

Sharp, Patrick B. 2014. "Questing for an Indigenous Future: Leslie Marmon Silko's *Ceremony* as Indigenous Science Fiction." In *Black and Brown Planets: The Politics of Race in Science Fiction*, edited by Isiah Lavender III, 117–30. Jackson: University Press of Mississippi.

Sheyahshe, Michael A. 2008. *Native Americans in Comic Books: A Critical Study.* Jefferson, NC: McFarland & Company.

Sheyahshe, Michael A. 2019. "Xenesi: The Traveler." Illustrated by Roy Boney Jr. In *Moonshot: The Indigenous Comics Collection,* edited by Elizabeth LaPensée and Michael Sheyahshe, 98–108. Vol. 3. Iqaluit, NU: Inhabit Education Books.

Simpson, Leanne Betasamosake. 2017. *As We Have Always Done: Indigenous Freedom through Radical Resistance.* Minneapolis: University of Minnesota Press.

Spiers, Miriam Brown. 2014. "Creating a Haida Manga: The Formline of Social Responsibility in *Red.*" *Studies in American Indian Literatures* 26, no. 3 (Fall): 41–61.

Spiers, Miriam Brown. 2021. *Encountering the Sovereign Other: Indigenous Science Fiction.* East Lansing: Michigan State University Press.

Starr, Arigon. 2012. *Super Indian.* Vol. 1. Illustrated by Arigon Starr. West Hollywood: Wacky Productions Unlimited.

Starr, Arigon. 2015a. *Super Indian.* Vol. 2. Illustrated by Arigon Starr. West Hollywood: Wacky Productions Unlimited.

Starr, Arigon. 2015b. "Ue-pucase: Water Master." Illustrated by David Cutler. In *Moonshot: The Indigenous Comics Collection,* edited by Hope Nicholson, 66–72. Vol. 1. Toronto, ON: Alternate History Comics.

Starr, Arigon. 2019. "Super Indian: Comic Book Blues." In *Dreaming in Indian: Contemporary Native American Voices,* edited by Lisa Charleyboy and Mary Beth Leatherdale, 58–59. Toronto, ON: Annick Press.

Stock, Richard. 2016. "Louise Erdrich's Place in American Literature: Narrative Innovation in *Love Medicine.*" *Prague Journal of English Studies* 5, no. 1: 119–39.

Storm, Jennifer. 2019. "Future World." Illustrated by Kyle Charles. In *Moonshot: The Indigenous Comics Collection,* edited by Elizabeth LaPensée and Michael Sheyahshe, 10–18. Vol. 3. Iqaluit, NU: Inhabit Education Books.

Teuton, Christopher B. 2010. *Deep Waters: The Textual Continuum in American Indian Literature.* Lincoln: University of Nebraska Press.

Thom, Ian M. 2009. *Challenging Traditions: Contemporary First Nations Art of the Northwest.* Vancouver, BC: Douglas & McIntyre.

Tiger, Yvonne N. 2019. "Indigenizing the (Final) Frontier: The Art of Indigenous Storytelling through Graphic Novels." *World Art* 9, no. 2: 145–60. https://doi.org /10.1080/21500894.2019.1638594.

Tso, Theo. 2015. *Captain Paiute,* no. 0. Illustrated and inked by Theo Tso. Albuquerque: Native Realities.

Tso, Theo. 2017a. *Captain Paiute,* no. 1. Illustrated by Theo Tso, lettered by Rob Schmidt. Albuquerque: Native Realities.

Tso, Theo. 2017b. "Why an Indigenous Superhero Is Needed?" Comic-book insert in *Captain Paiute,* no. 1, by Theo Tso, n.p. Albuquerque: Native Realities.

Tso, Theo. 2019. *Captain Paiute*, no. 2. Illustrated by Theo Tso, lettered by Rob Schmidt. Albuquerque: Native Realities.

Veregge, Jeffrey. n.d. "About Jeffrey. . . ." http://www.jeffreyveregge.com/about. Accessed June 12, 2023.

Veregge, Jeffrey. 2017. "Journeys." In *Moonshot: The Indigenous Comics Collection*, edited by Hope Nicholson, 130–43. Vol. 2. Toronto, ON: Alternate History Comics.

Veregge, Jeffrey. 2019a. "Salish Geek." In *Dreaming in Indian: Contemporary Native American Voices*, edited by Lisa Charleyboy and Mary Beth Leatherdale, 106–9. Toronto: Annick Press.

Vermette, Katherena. 2017. *Pemmican Wars*. Vol. 1 of *A Girl Called Echo*. Winnipeg, MB: Highwater Press, 2017.

Vermette, Katherena. 2018. *Red River Resistance*. Vol. 2 of *A Girl Called Echo*. Winnipeg, MB: Highwater Press.

Vermette, Katherena. 2020. *Northwest Resistance*. Vol, 3 of *A Girl Called Echo*. Winnipeg, MB: Highwater Press.

Vermette, Katherena. 2021. *Road Allowance Era*. Vol. 4 of *A Girl Called Echo*. Winnipeg, MB: Highwater Press.

Vernet, Camille. 2019. "Cole Pauls's Comics Preserve First Nations Language—And Also Celebrate Punks Eating Pizza." CBC, April 10, 2019. https://www.cbc.ca/arts/exhibitionists/cole-pauls-s-comics-preserve-first-nations-language-and-also-celebrate-punks-eating-pizza-1.5092379.

Vizenor, Gerald. 1992. "Ishi Bares His Chest: Tribal Simulations and Survivance." In *Partial Recall: Photographs of Native North Americans*, edited by Lucy R. Lippard, 64–71. New York: New Press.

Vizenor, Gerald. 2009. *Native Liberty: Natural Reason and Cultural Survivance*. Lincoln: University of Nebraska Press.

Ware, Chris. 2012. *Building Stories*. New York: Pantheon Books.

War Paint Studios. n.d. https://www.warpaintstudios.net/. Accessed August 6, 2020.

White, Hayden. 1987. *The Content of the Form: Narrative Discourse and Historical Representation*. Baltimore, MD: Johns Hopkins University Press.

Wolf, Werner. 2017. "Transmedial Narratology: Theoretical Foundations and Some Applications (Fiction, Single Pictures, Instrumental Music)." *Narrative* 25, no. 3 (October): 256–85.

Womack, Craig. 1999. *Red on Red: Native American Literary Separatism*. Minneapolis: University of Minnesota Press.

Yahgulanaas, Michael Nicoll. 2001. *A Tale of Two Shamans*. Pentiction, BC: Theytus Books; Haida Gwaii Museum at Qay'llnagaay.

Yahgulanaas, Michael Nicoll. 2009. *Red: A Haida Manga*. Madeira Park, BC: Douglas & McIntyre.

Yahgulanaas, Michael Nicoll. 2017. *War of the Blink*. Vancouver, BC: Locarno Press.

Yahgulanaas, Michael Nicoll. 2019. *Carpe Fin: A Haida Manga.* Madeira Park, BC: Douglas & McIntyre.

Younging, Gregory. 2018. *Elements of Indigenous Style: A Guide for Writing by and about Indigenous Peoples.* Edmonton, AB: Brush Education.

INDEX

Adare, Sierra S., 160n2
Afrofuturism, 58
Agoyo, Acee, 163n14
Aldama, Frederick Luis, 9, 23, 47,
   159n25; *Graphic Indigeneity*, 9
Aleiss, Angela, 172n25
Alexandratos, Jonathan, 172n22
Allen, Paula Gunn, 10, 84
Alvitre, Weshoyot, 6, 155n1; *Ghost River*,
   6, 85, 103–6, 152n8
Anderson, Eric Gary, 154n17
Anderson, Reynaldo, 57
Aquaman, 21, 156n5
Austin, Matt, 158n18

Baldy, Cutcha Risling, 163n16
Batman, 21, 26, 40, 44, 45, 49–50, 156n5,
   157n10
Bechdel, Alison, 136
Beltran, Robert, 160n2
Berila, Beth, 115–17, 142
Bernadin, Susan, 152n10, 170n12
Beyale, Shaun, 159n27
Black Panther, 21, 26, 157n7
Boney, Roy, Jr., 60, 64–67
Bray, Joseph, 114
Bray, Mark, 49–51, 160nn28–29
Brooks, Lisa, 84
Brown, Chester, 167n10
Brown, Jeffrey A., 51–52
Brownie, Barbara, 156n6
Bukatman, Scott, 23

Cage, Luke, 26, 157n7, 159n20
Captain America, 49–51, 156n6
Captain Marvel, 44
Carnes, Jeremy, 165n28
Carrington, André M., 58
Carston, Cynthia, 114
Chakotay, 160n2
Charles, Kyle, 60, 63–65
Chute, Hillary, 3, 114–15, 151n2, 156n4
Cohn, Dorrit, 168n17
Coogan, Peter, 25–26
Cooper, James Fenimore, 81
Cornum, Lindsey Catherine, 164n24
Cotter, Joshua W., 111
Cox, James H., 155n18
Crowsong, Richard, 60, 73–76, 79,
   164n19
Cutler, David, 60, 70–73, 155n1
Cyborg, 156n5

Dances with Wolves, 38, 158n17
Daredevil, 34, 44
Davis, Richard Paul. *See* Crowsong,
   Richard
DC, 4, 5, 7, 11, 21, 24, 39, 47, 145, 156n2,
   156n5
Deer Woman, 7
Deforest, Dale, 7
Deloria, Vine, Jr., 158n15
DeKoven, Marianne, 115, 169n5
Dembicki, Matt, 164n21
Dillon, Grace L., 58–59, 163n13, 163n15

Dimaline, Cherie, 11, 162n11, 166n5
Duff, David, 15
Donahue, James J., 7–8, 159n21, 159n24, 161n7, 162n9, 166n6, 169n3
Dragotta, Nick, 161n3
Dumont, Gabriel, 90, 100, 167n15

Ekedal, Rashan, 85
Erdrich, Louise, 10, 114, 166n5
Espinosa, Frank, 156n3
Estes, Nick, 84–85, 109
experimental comics: and audience interaction, 130–35, 140, 143; and culture, 120–27, 130–31, 137–42; and form, 111–17, 120–35, 136–43; and material culture, 130–32, 135–42, 172n22; and race, 115–16, 140–43; and technology, 136–42

Fantastic Four, 26
Fenton, Will, 103
Firefly, 15
Flash, the, 25, 145, 156n5
Francis, Consuela, 23
Francis, Dr. Lee, IV, 6–7, 153n10, 172n1; Ghost River, 6, 85, 103–6, 152n8
Fricke, Suzanne Newman, 160n1, 161n4
Frow, John, 15–17

Garroutte, Eva Marie, 38
Gateward, Frances, 13
Gavaler, Chris, 27, 156n2
genre studies, 14–17, 26–28, 145
Gibbons, Alison, 114
González, Christopher, 9–11, 22–23, 147, 156n3. See also narrative permissibility
Graydon, Danny, 156n6
Green, Vivien, 163n18
Green Arrow, 28
Green Lantern Corps, 26, 41
Grennan, Simon, 169n7

harris, eelonqa K., 115, 117, 135–43, 171nn19–20
Harris-Fain, Darren, 24
Harrison, Richard, 121, 126
Hatfield, Charles, 168n1
Henderson, Scott B., 14, 85, 95, 167n7, 167n13
Herman, Matthew, 148
Hickman, Jonathan, 161n3
Highwater Press, 5–6, 102, 146–48, 152n5, 167n14
Hill, Gord, 22, 25, 48–51; The Anti-Capitalist Resistance Comic Book, 48; The Antifa Comic Book, 49–51; The 500 Years of Resistance Comic Book, 48
historical comics: and education, 80, 86–102, 103–4, 166n4; and the Métis List of Rights, 90; and the Northwest Resistance, 91, 100; and race, 81–83; and time, 83–85, 86–95, 103–6, 161n4, 162n10, 166n6
Ho, Jennifer, 161n7
Houseman, Todd, 60, 61–63, 79, 145
Hughes, Ross, 158n18

Incredible Hulk, 34
Indigeneity, 18–19, 57
Indigenous futurism, 19, 58–61, 79, 160n1, 161n4, 163n18
Ishi, 36

Jae, Johnnie, 165n28
James-Perry, Elizabeth, 103, 152n8
Jennings, John, 13
Jerng, Mark C., 17
Johnson, Pauline, 100, 167n15
Jones, Stephen Graham, 22, 25, 51, 155n1, 172n2; My Hero, 44–48, 144, 159n23, 162n11, 163n15
Justice, Daniel Heath, 11, 12–13; Why Indigenous Literatures Matter, 12–13, 163n17

Kannenberg, Gene, 171n21
Kelp-Stebbins, Katherine, 130
Kilgore, DeWitt Douglas, 55–57, 161n8, 162n9
Kuhlman, Martha, 169n2

Lackaff, Derek, 153n12
language preservation, 76–77, 146–47
LaPensée, Elizabeth, 67–68, 77
Lavender, Isiah, III, 55, 161n5; *Black and Brown Planets*, 56, 163n13; *Race in American Science Fiction*, 55
Lee, Derrick B., 60, 73–76
Legion, 154n16
Levell, Nicola, 117–18
Librarie Drawn & Quarterly, 5
Lincoln, Kenneth, 10
Little Badger, Darcie, 155n1
Lockhurst, Roger, 53
Lodwick, Andrew, 167n7
Lothian, Alexis, 162n12
Lovett, Aaron, 159n23
Lowry, Chag, 85, 106–9, 145
Lukács, Georg, 80–82, 84, 166n2

Manifest Destiny, 12, 57
Marvel, 7, 11, 21, 39, 47, 155n1, 156n2. *See also* Marvel Cinematic Universe
Marvel Cinematic Universe, 4, 5, 7, 18, 21–22, 27, 44, 157n7
Masereel, Frans, 111
McHale, Brian, 114
Misha, 22, 161n5
Mistahimaskwa, 100–101
Momaday, N. Scott, 10, 11, 74, 84
Moonshot, 12, 60–73, 145, 147, 159n22, 160n1, 164n20
Morgan, Shaun, 161n7
Morris, Christine, 160n2

Nama, Adilifu, 157n11
narrative permissibility, 9–11, 22–23, 147

Native American Renaissance, 10, 22, 113, 155n17
Native Realities, 6–7, 147, 148, 153n11, 156n2, 173n4
Nodelman, Perry, 171n17
Norton Anthology of American Literature, 8

Oakenthorn, Tristen, 60, 73–76
Odjick, Jay, 22, 25, 40–42, 51, 158n18

Pagnucci, Gian S., 24
Park, Liz, 169n8
Pauls, Cole, 60, 76–78, 79, 146, 165n33
Peters, Shannon, 137
Polak, Kate, 82–83
Portage & Main Press, 5–6, 152n5. *See also* Highwater Press
Prince, Tommy, 98–100
Proudstar, Jon, 22, 25, 42–44, 51, 156n2, 159n22

Ramsay, John, 96–98
Renta, Kathryn S., 159n23
reservation politics, 27–28, 30–33; and water rights, 30–31
Rieder, John, 57
Riel, Louis, 90–91
Rifkin, Mark, 85, 162n10
Roanhorse, Rebecca, 58–59, 61, 163n14, 163n16
Robertson, David Alexander, 6, 14, 147, 172n2; *7 Generations*, 6, 167n16; *Tales from Big Spirit*, 6, 85, 95–102
Romagnoli, Alex S., 24

Salaris, Claudia, 164n18
Sales, Michael, 153n12
science fiction: and colonialism, 57, 66–67, 164n24, 165n28; and race, 53–58; and survivance, 54–55, 59, 63, 69, 76–79; and technology, 53–54,

59, 61–76; and time, 61–73, 161n4.
See also Afrofuturism; Indigenous
futurism
Scott, Sir Walter, 81
settler colonialism, 12–13, 19–20, 31,
52, 57, 60, 85, 118, 130; and blood
quantum, 38–39; and capitalism, 49,
70–71; and decolonization, 77, 81,
88–89; and environmental destruction, 60–65, 70–76, 165n28; and first
contact, 48–49, 59, 61–63, 68–70,
95–96; and reservation politics, 21–
22, 30–32, 33, 34–36, 55, 74, 156n6;
and technology, 18, 119; and time,
83–95, 109–10, 162n10; and violence,
42–44, 49–51, 61–63, 76–77, 82–83,
91–92, 96, 104–6, 162n9
Shaggy, Kayla, 146, 147; *The Sixth
World*, 146
Shannon, Ben, 61
Shantie, Ethan, 154n15
Sharp, Patrick B., 161n6
Shawnadithit, 95–96, 98
Sheyahshe, Michael, 60, 64–67, 79,
153n13, 172n24
Silence of the Lambs, The, 15
Silko, Leslie Marmon, 10, 22, 114, 116,
161n6, 166n5
Simpson, Leanne Betasamosake, 55,
153n11
Spider-Man, 26, 30, 44, 45
Spiegelman, Art, 168n1
Spiers, Miriam C. Brown, 54–55, 57,
126–31, 162n11, 170n13
Spurling, Elbe, 136
Starr, Arigon, 21–22, 25, 33–36, 38, 39,
51, 60, 79, 144, 158n13, 158n16, 172n2;
"Real Super Indians," 39–40; *Super
Indian*, 21, 24–25, 27, 33–40, 42, 44,
152n10, 158n12; *Tales of the Mighty*

Code Talkers, 145; "Ue-Pucase:
Water Master," 60, 70–73, 165n30
Star Trek, 53, 55, 68, 70, 160n2, 164n23,
165n27, 165n29
Star Wars, 53, 160n1
Stock, Richard, 114
Storm, Jennifer, 60, 63–65, 67, 79
Sulac, 159n23
superhero comics: and definitions,
25–28, 30–31, 39, 44–47, 156n4; and
exclusion, 21–25, 27, 44; and MPI
matrix, 25–26, 27, 30, 34, 40–42,
46–47; and politics, 27–28, 38–39,
48–51
Superman, 21, 25, 26, 36, 39, 44, 45,
49–50, 145, 156n5, 157n10
survivance, 11–12, 18, 54–55, 63, 76,
82–83, 88, 106–7, 126, 131

Tenascon, Patrick, 158n18
Teuton, Christopher B., 154n14
Thanadelthur, 101–2
Thom, Ian M., 120, 171n18
Tien, Wai, 167n7
Tiger, Yvonne N., 160n1
Tso, Theo, 7, 14, 21, 51, 153n12, 173n4;
Captain Paiute, 7, 21, 24–25, 27,
28–33, 42, 44, 147, 156n6, 157nn10–11

Van Camp, Richard, 6, 14; *Three
Feathers*, 6, 146
Veregge, Jeffrey, 60, 67–70, 79, 147,
155n1, 164nn22–23, 172n2
Vermette, Katherena, 14, 145; *A Girl
Called Echo*, 85–95, 110, 145, 167n11
Viola, Joshua, 159n23
Vizenor, Gerald, 10; and Ishi, 36,
158n14; *Native Liberty*, 11–12. See
also survivance
Vowel, Chelsea, 6

Ware, Chris, 111–13, 169n2
Welch, James, 8, 10, 22; *Fools Crow*, 8, 166n5
White, Hayden, 102–3, 168n18
Wilson, Daniel H., 145, 152n4, 156n1, 161n5, 162n11
Wolf, Werner, 171n15
Womack, Craig, 3
Wonder Woman, 21, 26, 49, 156n5

Yaciuk, Donovan, 85
Yahgulanaas, Michael Nicoll, 9, 14, 115, 117–35, 140, 142–43, 147, 172n2; and activism, 118–19, 132, 169n8, 170n9; and the formline, 121–30, 142, 170nn12–13; and Haida manga, 119–35, 169n7, 170nn10–11; and installation art, 117–19; *Red: A Haida Manga*, 9, 120, 121, 126–31, 135; *A Tale of Two Shamans*, 120–26, 131; *War of the Blink*, 131–35, 145
Yezbick, Daniel F., 172n22
Younging, Gregory, 151n1

ABOUT THE AUTHOR

Photo courtesy of the editor

James J. Donahue is author of *Contemporary Native Fiction: Toward a Narrative Poetics of Survivance* and *Failed Frontiersmen: White Men and Myth in the Post-Sixties American Historical Romance*, as well as coeditor of the collections *Narrative, Race, and Ethnicity in the United States, Post-Soul Satire: Black Identity after Civil Rights*, and *Greater Atlanta: African American Satire since Obama*. He is professor and assistant chair of the Department of English & Communication at SUNY Potsdam.

Printed in the United States
by Baker & Taylor Publisher Services